THE NARRATIVE OF THE
PERSECUTIONS OF AGNES BEAUMONT

THE NARRATIVE OF THE PERSECUTIONS OF AGNES BEAUMONT

Edited by
Vera J. Camden

Michigan State University Press
East Lansing

Early Women Writers 1650-1800: No. 1

ISBN 0-87013-505-8
Copyright 1992 and 1998 by Vera J. Camden

All Michigan State University Press books are produced on paper
which meets the requirements of American National Standard of
Information Sciences - Permanence of paper for materials
ANSI Z23.48-1984.

Michigan State University Press
East Lansing, Michigan 48823-5202

A Colleagues Book
Series Editor Robert Uphaus

Published originally by
Colleagues Press in 1992.

CONTENTS

ACKNOWLEDGMENTS

I should like to acknowledge the generous support of Dean Eugene Wenninger and the Kent State Research Council who, through research and travel grants, greatly facilitated this project. I should also like to thank Miss Patrica Bell of the Bedford County Archives for her generous assistance in sharing her biographical research into the life of Agnes Beaumont. The Bunyan Museum of Bedford kindly permitted me to use illustrations from their collection. For permission to view and reprint portions of the Agnes Beaumont manuscripts, I am also grateful to the British Library. And to Robert Uphaus of Colleagues Press I am grateful for sustained interest and support.

INTRODUCTION

AGNES BEAUMONT'S *A Narrative of My Persecutions* (1674) has in this century been remembered primarily as a footnote to Bunyan studies, an interesting glimpse into one of the various controversies which surrounded John Bunyan in his lifetime (see Furlong, 37–39). Agnes Beaumont was a member of Bunyan's congregation, devoted to his ministry and doubtless inspired by his example to compose a record of her persecutions. Her story is a *domestic* instancing of the principle projected by greater prophets of her day, who, like Bunyan, embrace imprisonment and even martyrdom rather than endure silencing. The drama of Bunyan's trial and imprisonment, recent in the minds of the Bedford congregation, clearly nourished Agnes Beaumont's vigorous self-advancement when she was called to defend herself before a local court. Similarly, Bunyan's recently published spiritual autobiography, with its haunting account of persecution and deliverance, must likewise have inspired her determination to inscribe the particulars of her ordeal in a written testimony. However indebted to Bunyan's life and work, Agnes Beaumont's narrative is, finally, a very different text from anything written by her famous pastor. With this new edition of her narrative I hope to revive interest in her text on its own merit. It is the legacy, the innovation and the life made manifest in Agnes Beaumont's brief account of her persecutions that this new edition hopes to bring out of obscurity and into the light of recent scholarship.

The Bedford Congregation and Its Beliefs

In 1672 Agnes Beaumont became a member of the Gamlinghay congregation of Bunyan's Independent Church in Bedfordshire (Church Book, 75). She was in fact the first member whose name was entered into the Church Book in Bunyan's own hand and one of the first to join under the pastorship which he assumed after his release from prison, under Charles II's Declaration of Indulgence. The Bedford Church had many sister congregations spread around the country, some at great distance. Its members, like Agnes Beaumont,

1

often walked or rode on horseback many miles to attend meetings at various gathering points. Bunyan himself traveled on horseback to minister to these distant members of his flock.

The First Independent Church at Bedford (Figure 1) was one of the many separatist churches which sprang up in resistance to the Established Church during the tumultuous years surrounding the English Revolution. The Bedford Church's origins, as the Church Book records, were humble. In 1650, twelve of the devout gathered together in "fellowship of the gospel" to begin "this Holy Work" (Church Book, 17); they chose John Gifford to be their pastor (see *Grace Abounding*, paras. 38, 77). The teachings and services of this church would reflect an apostolic purity, strict discipline, scriptural foundation in matters of church polity and a pared down, "democratic" ecclesiastical structure (Owens, xi). The doctrines of the Bedford Church were moderately Calvinist, tolerant in matters of baptism and communion, while adamantly predestinarian in their emphasis on the need for a calling and public testimony of conversion for its members (see Damrosch, 122). It is this last demand for a public testimony that sets the stage for both Bunyan's *Grace Abounding* and Agnes Beaumont's narrative. The language with which both describe the workings of God in their hearts is borne of the environment of intense self-scrutiny and then self-description which is fostered in the church.

From its very foundation in which eight of its original twelve members were female, the Bedford congregation's membership was predominantly made up of women. Agnes Beaumont would have found in these gatherings a place where women could find fellowship outside the home and, if not free to exercise real authority, might at least testify to the workings of God in their souls. It is here, in the living out of the Calvinist doctrines of the personal calling by God to the saint—whether male or female, slave or free—that Beaumont's narrative is engendered.

The Role of Women in Puritan England

A review of the seventeenth century's preoccupation with the patriarchy is fundamental to any full consideration of Beaumont's *A Narrative of My Persecutions*, because it is only against such a backdrop of the dissenting tradition and questions within that tradition that the

2

The first Bunyan Meeting (1707). *Courtesy of the Bunyan Museum, Bedford.*

significance of her text can be understood. Agnes Beaumont's story emerges from the tensions voiced in the debate over the analogy between the family and the state. She was born in that moment of British history when both the lower classes and women were writing themselves not necessarily into literary esteem but into testimonies of their personal salvation. When the logical and the expected course of spiritual experience is to translate one's subjectivity into salvific testimonies, it is not surprising that especially those women who followed this course should experience a new freedom. The traditional doctrines of woman's place which organized around images of subordination and service now find themselves reinterpreted as the scriptures surface, newly appropriated in living testimonies. Possession of the "logos" permits a possession of meaning, a taking hold of one's spiritual and physical destiny through the Word (Boyd and Berry, 50).

William Myers, one of the few scholars since G. B. Harrison to advance Beaumont's text, places her narrative in that group of "English writings at the close of the seventeenth century [which] registered and confirmed a deep-seated change in social and political relationships; they are marked with the anxieties of struggle, the assurance of victory, the experience of defeat" (27). He lays out the force of Agnes Beaumont's entrapment and fortuitous escape from the dilemma elucidated above: " . . . the Bible could divide the nation. It filled the minds of people like the younger Beaumonts . . . with so profound a sense of self that they were ready to defy paternal or state authority in its name" (7; see also Whiting, 122–123). It is exactly this sense of self in the face of domestic crisis which distinguishes Agnes Beaumont's narrative and sets her squarely in the tradition of the many female prophets who held the day during the Revolutionary years. "I pray you tell me," demands the dissenter preacher, Katherine Chidley,

> what authority [the] unbelieving husband hath over the conscience of his believing wife; it is true he hath authority over her in bodily and civil respects, but not to be a lord over her in conscience; and the like may be said of fathers and masters, and it is the same authority which the soveraigne hath over all his subjects and therefore it must needs reach to families . . . . (Chidley, 26)

4

Childley's insistent query, in its echo of Martin Luther's mandate that only Christ may be Lord and Master in the "bedchamber" of the believer's conscience, signals the extent to which the dissenter doctrines of free grace and the equality of believers pushed well beyond the church and the parliament, into the home. Chidley voices a controversy over patriarchy which preoccupied the social theorists of the seventeenth and eighteenth centuries. "All writers shared this preoccupation with the family as the fundamental unit of social relationships" (Hinton, 292). The Puritan's shattering refusal of the monarchy could not help but reverberate into the family and into philosophies of family rule. Keith Thomas writes that "the growth of sectarianism certainly seemed likely to provoke direct conflicts of loyalty within the family" ("Women," 335; see also Flandrin, 117–119). The point is not lost on contemporary critics of family patriarchy such as Mary Astell who, though herself a monarchist, turns John Locke's repudiation of the analogy between family and the state on a feminist edge.

> Is it not then partial in men to the last degree to contend for a practice of that arbitrary dominion in their families which they abhor and exclaim against in the state? . . . If all men are born free, how is it that all women are born slaves? (Stone 240; see Perry 150ff.)

According to Michael Walzer in his classic theory of the origins of radical politics, the Calvinist God is the "despot" behind the democratic urge expressed in such challenges to patriarchal hierarchy. "A despot destroys the structure of intermediate powers and makes possible a politics based on individual interests." The Calvinist God "overthrew kingdoms at a stroke, sent churches into precipitous decline . . . and bore the claims of no man" (152). But freedom, strictly speaking, was not the "Puritan purpose" (197). Once freed from the bonds of false religion, the saint must return to take up his or her place in the holy commonwealth and household government. This is the basis of Cromwell's regime.

But it is such a retrieval of traditional household governance that the woman saint often found as onerous as the burden of her previous spiritual ignorance. "Passive obedience," writes Mary Chudleigh, "you've transferred to us/ . . . that antiquated doctrine you disown,/

'Tis now your scorn and fit for us alone" (Stone, 240). Tyranny at home, because daily, close and unrelenting, was far worse than tyranny on the throne: "Nor is [arbitrary power] less but rather more mischievous in families than in kingdoms, by how much 100000 tyrants are worse than one" (Perry, 150). The situation for dependent children was not much different from that of women. If anything it was worse because as Sir Robert Filmer's treatise on patriarchy articulates, the "subordination of children is the *foundation* of all regal authority" (Hinton, 299, italics mine; see Schucking, 126; cf. Thompson, 86; Fraser, 264). "Men might dislike arbitrary power on a throne, but they welcomed it at home" (Nadelhaft, 577). The dilemma for the subordinate woman or child, then, was based on a paradox: in Christ, as a redeemed soul, she or he was called to freedom of worship, but at home was often forbidden that freedom (see Morgan, 78). Most of the church books and sermons of the period advise the dependent to disobey husbands or fathers rather than disobey the Lord (Thomas, 328; Bunyan, 1:167). This injunction became a powerful solvent to the patriarchy. Never before had willfulness been so "reinforced by piety" (Walzer, 194). Agnes Beaumont's narrative documents with rare spirit the paradox of this pious rebellion.

Her writing reveals the persistence of the spirit of dissent which had characterized the religious freedom of the 1640s. The congregations in Agnes Beaumont's time are quieter, of course, and the women are not prophesying and preaching in the numbers that they had formerly. The Restoration brought a general silencing of the feminist enterprises that were fermenting in these congregations (Hill, *Experience*, 21). Figures like Agnes Beaumont are thus all the more interesting, her drama all the more tenacious. And that she, like her pastor, takes her story to the saints suggests that the emergence of a *female* voice initially owed something at least to the very reformist doctrines which are later used — even in Bunyan's congregation — to silence women prophets. What Agnes Beaumont and other domestically enclosed women of the period discover is at least some transcendence of external restraint found in spiritual liberation. Women of this century would respond to the doctrines thus made more available to them in dissenting churches because these doctrines are exemplified in Christ's sufferings: their logic dictates a defiance of earthly authority still permitted by inward sovereignty and transcendence.

As late as 1683, in a movement which a critic as circumspect as William Tindall calls "feminist," Bunyan's women members are clamoring for separate prayer meetings. Tindall observes that, with "not unmerited abruptness," Bunyan wrote *A Case of Conscience Resolved* in which he reminds his women members that the memory of Eve and the "shame of their sex" should enforce spiritual dependency upon their minister and "keep them in their place" (56, 57). But the evidence of a text as compelling and spirited as Agnes Beaumont's suggests that the doctrines of free grace do emancipate the believer, male or female, from such mediation. And the scant evidence of church records hints at some movement among those church women who, like Bunyan, risked the consequences of remaining faithful to dissenting doctrines. If the price they paid was more often than not the disruption of domestic harmony, even this might lead — as it did with Agnes Beaumont — to a public forum. Familiar with revolt at home, she revels in outfacing her critics abroad; her narrative serves to divert herself and edify her readers well beyond the frights of persecution.

The History of the Narrative

Though written in 1674, a period still racked with controversy over the freedom of expression allowed to non-conformist congregations, Beaumont's narrative was not published until nearly one hundred years after it was written (1760), collected with a group of other testimonies, most written by daughters of clergymen. Beaumont's story is unusual, however, in that it is a fully realized narrative, fresh, with enough human detail and domestic flavor to set the spiritual drama firmly in the soil of English village life. The history of her text demonstrates that her primary audience was her church and her immediate community. There are two extant manuscripts of Beaumont's narrative in the British Library. The first (Egerton 2414), which is very likely the original copy, is written in a close, ill-educated hand, using eccentric spelling and punctuation and written "straight-on, without pauses or paragraphs" (Harrison, vi). (Figure 2) It seems to have had no title, no sense of formal presentation. The second manuscript (Egerton 2128), however, is a meticulously transcribed and slightly emended fair copy "Taken from a Coppy Transcribed from a MS.S. in the hands of Mrs.

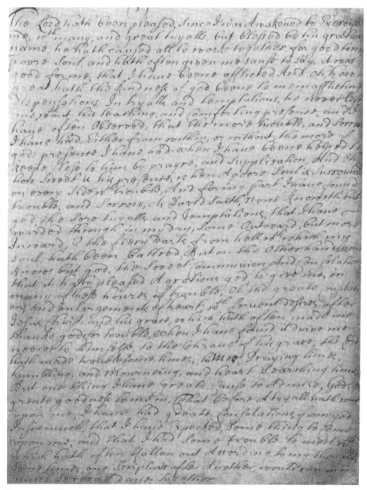

Figure 2. First page of original manuscript. *Courtesy of the British Library.*

Kenwick at Bavant in Hampshire."[1] (Figure 3) This copy confers upon the manuscript a formal presentation: it titles the narrative, names the author, identifying her first by her maiden name and then by her second husband, one Mr. Story "a merchant at High-Gate." The first page of text, additionally, reinforces the authorship of the narrative — "The Wonderful Dealings of God with Mrs. Agnes Beaumont, written by herself" — and decorates the page with a delicate pen and ink drawing of a local country scene. (Figure 4) The careful construction of this fair copy suggests not only the value which came to be placed on Agnes Beaumont's narrative within or shortly after her lifetime, but it also suggests something of the nature of the prepublication circulation of her writing: the extant fair copy being itself transcribed from a previous manuscript owned by Mrs. Kenwick. This would suggest that such valued narratives were copied and passed about the community of the faithful (Pomerleau, 22).

When Beaumont's narrative was published, it was collected along with some half dozen other narratives in a collection entitled, *An Abstract of the Gracious Dealings of God with Several Eminent Christians in their Conversions and Sufferings.* This volume went through ten editions, the last being in 1842. It became something of a nonconformist classic. In 1801, Reverend Samuel Burder, recognizing the peculiar interest and the "utility and acceptableness" of Agnes Beaumont's account, published her narrative separately, entitled "Real Religion: exemplified in the singular experience and great sufferings of Agnes Beaumont, of Edworth, in the County of Bedford." It was an inexpensive tract, meant to be "easily obtained by the poor . . . and a fit object of gratuitous circulation by the affluent." Her early editors took considerable liberty with Agnes Beaumont's prose in order to make the sense "complete"; in doing so they sacrificed much of the drama and originality of her style. The only modern edition of Beaumont's narrative (1929) was edited and introduced by G. B. Harrison, who recognized the narrative as a story "too good to be forgotten" (vii). This edition, now long out of print and circulation, was taken from the first manuscript in the British Library, and retains the eccen-

---

[1]Harrison mistakenly identifies the owner of the manuscript as a *Mr.* Kenwick.

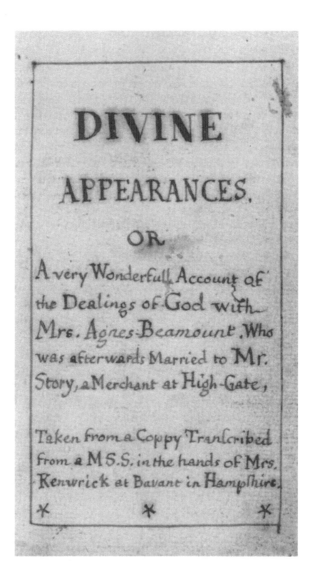

Figure 3. Fair copy manuscript title page. *Courtesy of the British Library.*

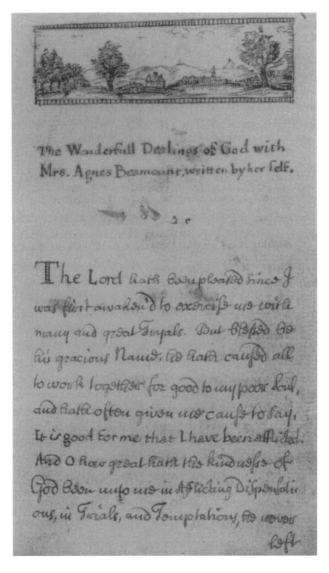

Figure 4. Pen and ink drawing from the fair copy manuscript. *Courtesy of the British Library.*

tric spelling of that copy, modernizing only the punctuation. I am much indebted to Harrison's edition. The present edition that follows, however, modernizes spelling and punctuation as these strictly mechanical divergencies from modern usage were considered distracting to the reader. No major changes have been made to the original text; this has meant that grammatical inconsistencies and crudities of style have been retained as features of Beaumont's conversational style and that biblical quotations have been kept as Beaumont remembered them even if they diverge somewhat from the Authorized Version.

Agnes Beaumont in Her Father's House

At twenty four [2] Agnes Beaumont lived with her widower father of fifty-nine — sharing the same chamber with him, sitting up with him in evenings, retiring when he went to bed, covering him, warming his bed, feeding him, keeping his fire, in short, serving him much like a wife. Strife interrupts the harmony of their home when Agnes insists on attending regular prayer meetings which take her from her home and from her devotions to her father. Strife turns to scandal when Agnes defies her father's command to abandon these meetings and rides to an evening prayer session on the back of John Bunyan's horse. The two talk of the ways of the Lord as they ride along. But sparks of gossip spread into flames of accusations by neighbors who report to her father that Agnes is being seduced by her married pastor. Agnes's father, in a rage at her disobedience, locks her out of the house in the dead of winter. She sleeps in the barn that night, with the mud and ice of her journey freezing on her boots. She is forbidden to return home and threatened with being cut off from her inheritance if she does not promise to abandon her religious assembly. In desperation she yields. Two days later her father dies of a heart attack at the age of fifty-nine. Agnes is accused of poisoning him and of conspiring with John Bunyan in this murderous exploit. A coroner and jury are brought in

---

[2] Agnes was twenty-two when she joined the congregation of Bedford in 1672; her father died in 1674, making her twenty-four at the time of this crisis.

from a neighboring village and she is acquitted of all charges. Her
accuser, a rejected suitor, is exposed to the shame of his own false and
scheming testimony. This *is* too good a story to be forgotten, as G. B.
Harrison said in 1929. But the significance of her narrative extends beyond its interest
as a rustic yarn. Beaumont's capacity to engage her audience and
characterize her plight before a court of law saved her from being
burned at the stake. What is remarkable about Beaumont is that,
though a woman, she followed Bunyan's model: she silenced her per-
secutors in a community courtroom rather than lapse into the exemplary silence of the woman and she recorded her triumph for the
saints. Equally notable, Beaumont does not in her prose follow the
basic pattern of female autobiography set up by the tradition of the
conversion testimony.[3] She does not apologize for writing or for being
a poor ignorant woman in the manner which virtually defines women's
autobiographical writing well into the eighteenth century and beyond
(Heilbrun, 16, 17). She has so interiorized the English Bible that the
suggestion of various verses becomes a kind of second language, a key
to unlock her psychological and spiritual states. As her early editor, the
Rev. Burder, proclaims in his notes to her text: "Who can forbear to
remark the passages which were all along brought to the mind of this

---

[3]N. H. Keeble's article on the "Feminine in the thought and work of John
Bunyan" concludes that "Divine and masculine perceptions happily agree in
finding women loveliest when most sensitive to their lesser status and their
inherited guilt: the more modesty and shame in their bearing in acknowledge-
ment that 'by the woman sin came into the world', 'the more beautiful they
are to both God and men' " (*Works*, 3: 673a). Agnes Beaumont's testimony,
however, demonstrates in its almost brazen self-vindication that the doctrines
of free grace which inspirited Bunyan's defiance of authority at least permitted
her the courage of self-defense and even self-celebration.
  While Agnes Beaumont's narrative of persecution exhibits many of the
features found in New England women's captivity narrative, sharing both their
consolation to the afflicted and their biblical typology of forbearance in the
face of affliction, it is crucial to highlight Agnes Beaumont's self-vindication.
Instead of the traditional feminine disclaimers, Agnes Beaumont offers her
jury and the audience of her narrative no passive forbearance against the
hollow accusations of her accusers but, rather, a routing of their intentions
(Kolodny, 97–101).

gracious woman?" He sees her facility with the scriptures as one more proof of the piety of this woman who, because she was once accused, does in some sense *need* to be "proved" perpetually.[4]

But for modern readers Beaumont's gift for story telling does more than entertain or edify. Because it is so personal, so localized and so articulate, her narrative takes its place today as one extremely valuable inlet into the seventeenth–century family at a time when the study of the family as an institution has perhaps never been more vital (e.g., Bosse, 6,7; Sharpe, 30; Pollock, 262–271). Neither fiction nor conduct book nor conversion narrative, Beaumont's narrative of her persecutions emerges as an unusually candid record of a domestic crisis. This crisis becomes all the more interesting to contemporary scholarship as it contributes to the current "drive to exhume the culturally suppressed narrative of the father and daughter" (7). In what is surely one of the most interesting critical contributions to this drive, Linda Bosse argues in her essay, "The Father's House and the Daughter in It," that "relative to incest and kinship structures . . . culture has been built on the relationship it has seemed least eager to discuss—that between father and daughter." Indeed, for all of the spate of "family" studies in various fields, the father-daughter relationship has "been written all over by tacit injunctions that have forbidden its charting." "[I]nvisible commandments. . . demarcate the father-daughter territory and prohibit discursive entrance into it" (20, 21). The historical as well as psychological significance of Beaumont's account, then, derives in part from the fact that she charts with remarkable intensity her struggle within this very territory. Her urge for self-disclosure and self-

---

[4]For the Puritans and their religious heirs, it is by the spiritual force of one's language, the wedding of God's Word to one's heart and mind, that true election and calling are measured. "[N]o parts of scripture could be better adapted to her ease and circumstances throughout the whole of her troubles. And may not this be esteemed one evidence of their being sealed in her heart by the spirit of the Lord?" (Burder, 11). See Whiting's review of Beaumont's story and his assurance of her "goodness" (123). Keeble explores Bunyan's extreme, "almost obsessive" denial of guilt in the Agnes Beaumont incident, seeing in Bunyan's repudiation of women a traditional identification of the woman with temptation and destruction.

14

vindication affords us a window into the largely uncharted territory of the daughter-father relationship.

Agnes Beaumont's narrative of self-vindication is first a narrative of persecutions; it reflects the absolute dependency and vulnerability that characterized a daughter of her class and condition in this period. She dramatizes the tenacity of her father's determination to keep her enslaved as his caretaker. But she also reveals what she, along with droves of the dissenters, had discovered in churches like Bunyan's: in Christ she is free. The doctrine of free grace, the assertion of the spiritual equality of all believers, and the sense of individual integrity consequent on the assurance of a direct relationship with God, nurtured the independence which leads to the victory she recounts in the narrative.

Agnes's solitary existence in a farm house, an existence which might otherwise deaden both identity and aspiration, is enriched by hours of prayer. She has learned from her pastor how to make God the companion of her days. When Bunyan in his Preface to *Grace Abounding* asks the congregation for whom his testimony was intended, "Have you forgot the close, the milk house, the stable, the barn and the like where God did visit your soul?", it is as if Agnes Beaumont responds in her own testimony that, far from forgetting God's presence, He is the one certain hope of her existence. The spirit of the Lord inhabits the world she walks through. "A corner in the house, or barnes, or cowhousen, or stable or close, under the hegges, or in the wood"—all are places which ring with the songs of grace. The meetings of fellow believers become a communion in the midst of her cloistered existence with an aging father. He, not surprisingly, resists her attending these gatherings, yet she fights for the freedom to go, declaring "it was like death to be kept from such a meeting." The meetings (Figure 5) provide her with an identity separate from the domestic domination of her father. John Beaumont's enraged resistance to her new freedom culminates when Agnes happily takes a seat on Bunyan's horse on the way to church. Her father's jealousy reveals a woundedness at her obvious devotion to the young minister (see Furlong, 37, 38).

Beaumont's description of her father's feelings later in the narrative makes it clear that she feels his rivalry with Bunyan and the Bedford congregation, as well as his anxiety over her sexual exploitation. John Beaumont is most susceptible to rumors of Bunyan's sexual adven-

Figure 5. Bunyan preaching in St. Paul's Square, Bedford. *Courtesy of the Bunyan Museum, Bedford.*

tures. "But it was my riding behind John Bunyan, he said, that vexed him. . . . [T]hat evil minded man in the town would set him against the meetings . . . [saying] 'These be they that lead silly women captive into houses and for a pretense make long prayers.' "[5] (Figure 6) To the modern reader the scandal and gossip which surrounded a mere horseback ride may seem absurd but it would not have seemed so to Agnes Beaumont's contemporaries. It was, in fact, not uncommon at all for folks to engage in all manner of sexual activity while riding horseback; her ride would, in that sense, have represented to her community an outrageous carnal opportunity.[6]

Agnes is attractive, dramatic, articulate. We know from her account that she refused one suitor (now her accuser, Mr. Feery) and has likely dismissed others; yet, at twenty–four she is precariously close to remaining single and must therefore be perceived as a threat to her community. Judging from contemporary church records and ordinances, it is likely that the option of remaining single was presenting itself to some of the young women in these dissenter sects. Among the Fenstanton baptists, for instance, it was ruled unlawful to keep an unmarried daughter at home for fear of the danger of her idleness: she

---

[5]G. B. Harrison remarks that the 'abundant hearsay' of the community as to Bunyan's evil doings (see *Grace Abounding*, 306–317) might well have caused John Beaumont anxiety for his daughter and may explain Bunyan's reluctance to carry her.

W. R. Owens similarly ascribes these passages which were added to the fifth edition of Bunyan's autobiography (1680) to his indignation over the Beaumont affair. "Bunyan was deeply disturbed by the affair, as can be seen from the sequence of twelve paragraphs, vehemently rebutting allegations of an illicit relationship with her or any woman . . ." (xviii).

[6]"A girl riding behind a man on the same horse was one . . . common catalyst to village gossip. A kind neighbor, picking up one of the village girls returning from market, found himself threatened by the girl's father because this innocent act had been the 'cause of a fame in the parish concerning his daughter'. . . . The close physical contact provided by the sharing of a horse's back created sexual opportunities, especially for mutual, manual stimulation. . . . The male genitals were a not uncommon substitute for the pommel with many a female pillion passenger. Conversely, a Weare man carried a woman 'beside him upon his horse . . . and did feel her by the privy members twenty times by the way'" (Quaife, 48, 49). I am greatful to Professor Ted Underwood for drawing this historical material to my attention.

17

Figure 6. Bunyan on horseback assaulted by an old woman. *Courtesy of the Bunyan Museum, Bedford.*

must either be married and kept under her husband's rule, or put out to service (Hill, *World*, 376). The reality of confinement under the authority of husband or father is one of the persistent (if not always explicitly enunciated) traumas of the spiritual and secular autobiographies written by women in this period. Mary Rich, Countess of Warwick, writes of her domestic plight, "I was hindered by my lord's commands from going to church, for which I was most troubled, seeing him so passionate about it." This same lord cuts down all the trees in the grove surrounding their home because it is the place where Mary Rich seeks solitude to meditate and pray (Findley and Hobby, 20).

While John Beaumont's fears of Bunyan's motives are transparently those of an anxious father, he rightly senses that his daughter's intense admiration for Bunyan constitutes an expression of her womanhood. Her "distraction" is the distraction of the lover: "Seeing me in such distress about my soul, [he] . . . would say to some neighbors. . .: 'I think my daughter will be distracted, she scarce eats, drinks, or sleeps; and I have lived these three score years and scarce ever thought of my soul.' " He is furious at his daughter's violation of his authority. "So I followed him about the yard as he went to serve the cows; but he would not hear me. The more I entreated him, the more angry he was with me, and said I should never come within his doors again, unless I would promise him never to go to a meeting again as long as he lived." The classical Oedipal dynamic is evident in her account. Agnes Beaumont's new affiliation with Bunyan, with the people of God, and with Christ himself establishes a rivalry that offers her an opportunity to break the Oedipal bond and fulfill her womanhood outside her father's domain.

Recent feminist scholarship, however, would suggest that perhaps more deeply embedded in this sort of narrative situation is the largely neglected dimension of the father's seduction of the daughter, an elaboration on the classical Oedipal situation in which the child's desire is paramount. *Oedipus at Colonus* is a play which, from the standpoint of the daughter, deserves perhaps as much analysis as *Oedipus Rex* does from the standpoint of the son. The daughters at Colonus were "born to nurse" their father; like Lear's Cordelia, the daughter here is seduced into a maternal role by a logic which permits the father an "attempt to reconstruct his lost union with the mother, an adult reversion to infantile dependency to which women—and in particular daughters—are expected to respond" (Bosse, 41ff.). With no superior father to provide interdiction within the family, the only threat comes from rival males—brothers and suitors. Such an elaboration on the traditional Oedipal myth illuminates Agnes Beaumont's story: her mother's death when she was only ten years old and her status as the the youngest child could only set the stage for the elder John Beaumont's evident dependency on his adult daughter by the time the incident with Bunyan occurs. Her collusion, resistance and finally despair in the face of all this too literal Oedipal entanglement provides the urgency in her narrative.

Because of John Beaumont's jealous anger, Bunyan himself at first refuses Beaumont the ride. "If I should carry you, your father should be grievous angry with me." But Agnes's and her brother's supplications persuade him. She gloats over her accomplishment. "My heart was puffed up with pride, and I began to have high thoughts of my self and proud to think I should ride behind such a man as he was; and I was pleased that anybody did look after me as we rode along." John Beaumont insists that his daughter "leave off going after that man." He broods over her devotion to the married Bunyan; he attempts to yank her from the horse. But she will not abandon her meetings; she substitutes obedience to a heavenly father for obedience to her earthly father. The doctrines of the Bedford church insist on such a substitution. She must separate from her father's enclosure of her will. "Father, said I, you can't answer for my sins, nor stand in my stead before god, I must look to the salvation of my soul, or I am undone forever."

Like Bunyan himself who resisted the fathers of the Established Church, Beaumont resists patriarchal authority to obey her conscience. In doing so she is, in fact, adhering to Bunyan's explicit directions to his followers. In "A Few Sighs from Hell," he mocks the complaint of the fearful child: "Oh, saith another, I would willingly go in this way but for my father; he chides and tells me he will not stand my friend when I come to want; *I shall never enjoy a pennysworth of his goods; he will disinherit me*" (167, italics mine). The dissenting congregation's emphasis on the individual's obedience to his or her conscience clearly upset the structure of authority in the home. Again, Keith Thomas writes, "We must not underestimate the importance of sectarian claims to limit the father's authority in the sphere of conscience, for it was precisely the supposedly divine origin of his position and his role as household priest which had mattered in the family" (335). Bunyan himself was sensitive to power in the home as analogous to political rule; when he rails against landlords, he rails against husbands and fathers.

> Interestingly though, ungodly landlords were generally classed by Bunyan along with other heads of smaller communities, those of individual households rather than villages. He railed equally against 'mad brain'd blasphemous husbands that are against the godly and chaste conversation of their wives; . . . If you love your own souls, your tenants souls, your wives souls, your servants souls, your childrens souls . . .'

then, argues Bunyan, give them freedom of worship" (Spufford, 307, quoting Bunyan, "Sighs" 1:56).

In his study of the Puritan family, Levin L. Schucking concludes from his reading of conduct books of the period, that the severity within the Puritan home was so inhibiting to the bonding between family members that it virtually precluded, for instance, "personal relationship" between siblings (88–90). The point about Agnes Beaumont's narrative in this regard is that the naive realism of her account belies the formality of the conduct books with a real case of a family in crisis. Agnes Beaumont is not put out to service, but serves her father; the brother, far from refusing to undermine the father's authority, attempts to usurp that authority in the name of the Lord. This little book illustrates far more vividly than the formal strictures of conduct books, sermons and other such treatises the human dimensions of a family crossed by competing structures of authority.[7]

Indeed, the human dynamic is never far from the surface of this

---

[7]Margaret Ezell's study of the history of the family cites the important distinction between theory and practice in the domestic settings of early modern England. She cautions against relying too heavily on "literary evidence" such as conduct books and similarly idealized portraits of Christian behavior. She advances instead documents such as letters, diaries, journals, etc., in her reconstruction of the family in history.

narrative. John Beaumont is, for instance, much more angry with the entreaties of others on behalf of his daughter than he is with the young woman herself. And her brother, John—who himself had in 1669 been accused by the churchwardens of Edworth of refusing to take the sacrament in his parish church (Harrison, ix; Myers, 98)—seems only to aggravate the father's rage. He becomes a provocation as he attempts to exert some rival claim to authority over her goings-on. Indeed, Agnes Beaumont is so consistent in her report of both her and her father's rejection of the younger John Beaumont's intervention in the tumult that one wonders if he is not, in fact, perceived as "taking over" the father's authority. If the servants in the son's house used to serve their "Old Master," John Beaumont the elder, then the danger seems clear. Will she, too, be expected to join her brother's household rather than stay in her father's home?[8] For whatever reason, Agnes Beaumont repudiates her brother's help and is reluctant, that first night, to seek shelter in his home (as her father had assumed she had done). She resists her brother's protection almost as fiercely as she resists her father's demands. She records "to" the audience of her narrative (in asides and unspoken thoughts) her resentment of his intrusion. Her writing itself thus affords her, among other things, a voice outside the traditional constraints imposed by the structure of her household position.

But the struggle to break free from that domain is tinged with guilt and remorse. Though the embrace of the Lord exacts the relinquishing of the father, she is anxious about breaking his patriarchal authority. "I was grieved to think I should lose my fathers love for going to seek after Jesus Christ." But the break constitutes a long stretch of self-exertion. In the midst of her guilty fear, as she is locked out by her earthly father, she has recourse to her heavenly father. The substitution is constant and serves a crucial psychological function. "Pray to thy father that seeth in secret, and thy father that seeth thee in secret

---

[8]John Beaumont the younger is listed in the Bedford Historical Record as possessing the largest house in the village of Edworth; like Agnes's older sister Joan, John received only one shilling in his father's will, indicating that both had already received their inheritance—he to set up the stock and equipment of his farm and she as a dowry.

shall reward thee openly." And again, when grieved at the loss of her father's love, she is reminded of her creator: "The father himself loveth you." It is this assurance that challenges—almost defeats—the patriarchal hold. Ultimately, however, her economic dependence plunges Beaumont back into abject obedience to her father's demands.

Her account of the battle of wills between herself and her father when she attempts to return home after the meeting becomes the dramatic centerpiece of her narration. Her break from his threats is not easy: she is readily locked into a masochistic tenacity in her attempts to regain his favor. She lies at his feet for mercy, tricks him into opening the door, struggles against him physically and pockets the house key when he is not looking. He threatens to throw her into the pond, forces the key from her with his threats and then taunts her with the key, offering it only in exchange for her promise. They stand outside the barn trembling in the cold, locked in conflict.

> So many times together he held the key out to me, to see if I would promise him; and as often I refused to yield . . . at last he began to be impatient; "Hussy," said he, "what doe you say? If you will promise me never to go to a meeting again as long as I live, here is the key; take it, and go in"; and held the key out to me. (58)

His taunting and threats finally break her down. The economic reality of her dependence prevails over her preference for the company of the holy. Beaumont records his most grievous threat: it is an echo of Bunyan's caveat preached nearly ten years earlier.

> only this one thing he said, he would never give me a penny as long as he lived; nor when he died, but he would give it to them he never saw before. . . . [A]t the hearing of it my heart began to sink . . . . "What will become of me? To go to service and work for my living is a new thing to me; and so young as I am too. What shall I do?" (52)

The message of spiritual autonomy has provided a separateness and an integrity: she tries to hope on an eternal inheritance. But the economic reality of her dependence tests and breaks that freedom. Beaumont's submission profoundly depresses her: "Now I see what all my resolutions were come to. This was Sabbath day night, a black night." Once she is safely in his house, her father moves from his rage to an unbridled grief at the suffering he has caused her. "He wept like a child . . . . and told me how troubled he was for me that night he shut me out" (61). But then he cheerfully reassigns her the nursing role. He was, she reports, "very loving to me, and bade me get him some supper; which I did. . . . Thus I went groaning about till I was almost spent; and when my father was but gone out of the house, I made the house ring with dismal cries" (59, 60). Like Bunyan who "sold his Savior," Beaumont fears she has gained Esau's mess of pottage—her father's inheritance—while losing her soul. " 'Now,' thought I, 'if my father could give me thousands of gold what good would it do me?' " (60). We might suspect that Beaumont's depression is rooted in more than her separation from the Bedford church. It is additionally due to her grief over all that she imagines she has lost in losing the church—not just spiritual fellowship but the subjectivity that is suppressed under her father's domain. The point cannot be overstated: the gatherings of these local churches provided women an outlet for themselves by getting them out of the house.[9]

John Beaumont's fatal heart attack two days later, of course, plunges Agnes into further guilt. She imagines his sickness stemmed from her neglect of his meals and fire. As she runs for help she imagines "rogues" running after her in the night, waiting to knock her over the head. This anxiety is somewhat alleviated by her recollection of a prophetic dream she had received three months prior in which a great, aged apple tree topples over. In her dream Beaumont tries to restore the old tree to life but it decays—craggy roots exposed, subject to time and the elements, while around it younger saplings sprout, blossom, flourish. She takes this dream for prophecy; we may also take it for wish-fulfillment. Agnes Beaumont eagerly embraces youth while her aging father collapses from the strain of reining her in. John Beaumont was no match for his daughter in this crisis; he suffered the

---

[9]Rural women were generally enjoined not to keep company with neighbors except on feast days and other assemblies. This, coupled with the reality of household duties, meant that the country woman of early modern England was confined to the house and not given opportunities to participate in the community (Shammus, 3–24).

consequences of uncontrolled apoplexy. January cannot win May. But Agnes feels responsible for a death her dream desired. Agnes's vulnerability in the community as well as the home is highlighted by the aggravation of her rejected suitor Mr. Feery's campaign against her. He accuses Agnes of patricide—a capital offense—on no more certain evidence than his own bitter resentment, proclaiming "she must be burned." Beaumont reveals at the end of her narrative the failed courtship strategy of Mr. Feery of some three years earlier. His failure then accounts for his current strategy of revenge.

> Now my father's will was made three years before he died, and Mr. Feery made it. And then he put my father on to give me more than my sister because of some design that he had then, but afterwards when I came to go to meetings he was turned against me. (82)

Here again recent research on the role played by conflicts over inheritance rights in Puritan New England witch trials is suggestive. Women, especially single women who stood to inherit fortunes of whatever size, were as vulnerable to accusations as the more familiar cases of the disenfranchised poor and elderly woman. In subtle and intricate ways, "anxieties about inheritance were at the heart of most witchcraft accusations" (Karlsen, 84, 196). Agnes Beaumont's status as a single woman due to inherit some money is indeed both threatening and tantalizing. It would seem that Beaumont's rejection of the unconverted Mr. Feery involves not merely a refusal of his advances but, more importantly, a refusal of an arrangement set up between him and her father, whereby she will inherit a larger portion of his estate than her siblings. Her enhanced inheritance had served as tempting dowry gift for Mr. Feery. But her conversion undermines not only the scheme but also the psychology of the dowry bestowal: "The bestowal design places the daughter's departure from the father's house and her sexual union with another male into a text defined by obedience to her father—not preference for an outside male" (Bosse, 32). The rage felt by the elder John Beaumont at his daughter's following Bunyan thus belies the full subversion effected by her position.

The persecution of Agnes Beaumont by Mr. Feery thus follows the well-established pattern of witch trials. Vulnerable women without male protection were accused of crimes and sorcery by those in the community whose own guilt for crimes against the women gives rise to projected accusation (Demos, 150–210). While Mr. Feery's greedy revenge is clear to her judges, Agnes is, notwithstanding, threatened with burning and brought to court. "I knew myself clear, . . . Thought I, 'Suppose God should suffer my enemies to prevail, to take away my life; how shall I endure burning? . . . But the thoughts of burning would sometimes shake me all to pieces" (74). Beaumont's control of her fear and her determination to face both her accuser and the jury are crucial to her survival. "Thought I, if they should see me dejected and look daunted, they would think I was guilty." In the face of an admitted inferiority before her judges, she nevertheless stands in the "the Spirit" – "So I was helped to look my accuser in the face with boldness."

A less attractive defendant might have indeed been burned (Harrison, xviii). But Agnes Beaumont is acquitted. The coroner angrily condemns Mr. Feery for his baseless rumblings. "You have taken away her good name from her, and you would have taken away her life from her if you could"(80). He repeatedly calls Agnes "sweetheart," takes her by the hand and assures her that God will provide a husband for her despite the "malice of this man." The coroner remarks that had Mr. Feery given Agnes five hundred pounds, it would not have been just compensation for her persecution at his hands.[10] The reality is, however, that Mr. Feery is not penalized for his slander; in fact, he proceeds to stir up trouble between Agnes and her brother-in-law over her father's will. To stave off another law suit, Agnes surrenders to her sister "three score pounds for peace and quietness." Village life being what it is, of course, peace and quiet are not that easily restored. Slander continues to spread but she marches through the marketplace inhabited by gossips still determined to outface her enemies. "So I walked through and through the market . . . And I saw some cry, and some laugh. 'Oh,' thought I, 'mock on; there is a day coming will clear all' " (83).

Beaumont's pious readers find in her strut through the marketplace some remnant of that carnal pride which she took in mounting John Bunyan's horse in the first place. "If there is one small thing in her

---

[10]See Sharpe, 32, 33 on the role of the coroner and "neighborly scrutiny" in the control of family affairs; see also Keith Thomas, *Religion*, 526–530.

noble behavior which might be criticized," writes one chaste observer, "it is her visit to the market after the ordeal was over to outface her critics." The Christian may not, they say, "court the smile of the world" (Lupton, 49). But Beaumont's parade is really the essential impulse behind her spirit of testifying. It derives from the energy released when she breaks the Oedipal bond. It persists in her self-defense before the carnal men of the court, in her contemptuous indictment of her mercenary suitor *and* in her final written narrative. Christ's cause legitimizes her public drama as well as her desire: "Sister," says Agnes's brother John, "you are now brought upon the stage to act for Christ and his ways." Her text is no more and no less than the culmination of her dramatic calling. From it she gains all of the narcissistic rewards delivered by spiritual testimonies, however humbly they may be delivered by the "chief of sinners." Instead of being burned into infamy in martyrdom, she justified her sainthood and enjoyed the fame of her self-fashioning narrative. More to the point, she enjoyed the *telling* of her tale: "I could not but tell this news to several myself, and it did serve to divert me sometimes." It is this level of enjoyment which accounts, I suspect, for G.B. Harrison's desire to preserve this odd testimony because "it is a remarkable piece of natural prose writing" (vii).

* * *

Agnes Beaumont's narrative surely calls into question such generalizations as offered by Lawrence Stone who argues that the daughter in the seventeenth-century family may be "regarded as no more than a tiresome drain on economic resources." This text suggests that whatever her tenuous economic position may have been, the seventeenth century daughter is also inscribed into a text of desire by which her loss to the father may become loss of himself (Bosse, 46). Much more useful than Stone's improbable portrayal of the daughter's negative consequence is Michel Foucault's conclusion that since the seventeenth century, the family and sexuality become sites at which the public and private intersect (Haeny-Peritz, 186; Foucault, 110). What this means in the context of Beaumont's narrative is that her text becomes an exemplary transition piece: it partakes of the confessional discourse concerned with sin and salvation we have come to expect in the Puritan tradition, while at the same time it invites the reader's "identification" through its novelistic design of reproducing the subject of desire. Agnes Beaumont possesses the native wit of the *raconteur*. Assaulted by both father and would-be suitor over the disposition of her heart and her inheritance, Agnes finds deliverance through the Lord and His people. Though not a fiction, in its own way hers is a very Richardsonian tale of sexual intrigue, filial disobedience, personal anguish and public vindication; here is the country girl's own version of virtue in distress and virtue rewarded: the self triumphant, Puritan style.

Addressing the problem of the "woman's domain" in relation to cultural hegemony, Nancy Armstrong remarks that "political events cannot be understood apart from woman's history, from the history of woman's literature, or from changing representations of the household"(10). The writing of Agnes Beaumont reveals the intersection of the political and the domestic in rural England of the late seventeenth century. The community still exerts its authority in interpreting and resolving the crisis of the Beaumont household. Agnes Beaumont's chronicle is *public*, written before that time in British history when, by Armstrong's and others' account, novel writing "invaded, revised, and contained the household by means of strategies that distinguished private from social life and thus detached sexual from political history. On the domestic front, perhaps even more so than in the courts and the marketplace, the middle class struggle for dominance was fought and won" (19; see Spenser, 15; Todd, 95–96). Agnes Beaumont starts her vindication in the courtroom only to take herself literally into the marketplace to display the ease of conscience and the power given to her by a sense of righteousness, poise and personal freedom.

As an example of what Felicity Nussbaum calls an "emergent form," Beaumont's narrative then may be brought from the periphery to the center of critical consideration as it is precisely in these forms that the fissures, the gaps in the dominant ideologies of class, gender and genre can be seen. In these terms, Beaumont's text participates in all of the individuality of the emerging bourgeois self, while it marks her position within the discourse of Puritan theology. Within this theology she must display her conscience and her spiritual experience to prove her election. But she must also, in order to survive, demonstrate her subjugation within the domestic sphere with enough finesse and native wit to resolve these conflicting demands in "publishing" her family crisis. In her text, the public and the private indeed intersect at the point of the family and sexuality. Her narrative becomes in its self-writing "part of the conquest over meaning and the contest over the power to have the real" (Nussbaum, xxi). Agnes Beaumont's conquest is over the truth; her version of the real must win out in order to save her life.

Beyond the Narrative: The Rest of Her Life

The life thus saved for Agnes Beaumont did not evidently turn out as the coroner had predicted: she did not marry in her youth. Indeed, Agnes's father would appear to have been correct if his worry was that her outrageous behavior in going after Bunyan would ruin her chances of marriage. Whether it was for this or for the scandalous accusations leveled at her by Mr. Feery or, indeed, for her own reasons, Agnes Beaumont did not marry until middle age. Very recent archival research[11] discovered that the tradition which had her marrying a Bedfordshire farmer in her youth was wrong. Her first marriage (1702) was at age fifty to a Thomas Warren, a land-owning gentleman who, having no children, divided his estate upon his death (1707) between his wife Agnes and his cousins. In 1708 she joined with his other legatees in selling his estate and married her second husband, one Samuel Story, a London fishmonger of considerable property and, according to Isaac James, "great seriousness." This marriage lasted until Agnes's death in 1720. Nothing is currently known about her life between the years 1692 and 1702 but it is obvious that she was not raising a family. We know that her brother John (who in 1671 had the largest house in the village of Edworth) lived nearby, as did her sister in all likelihood; another brother, William, worked as a successful

---

[11]I am indebted for most of the biographical detail which follows to the archival research of Miss Patrica Bell of the Bedford County Historical Society, who shared with me her recent investigations into the life of Agnes Beaumont.

vintner and lived in London. So until her first marriage, it seems likely that Agnes Beaumont would have lived on her inheritance in her father's house.[12] We know that she asked to be buried near the minister John Wilson in the Meeting House Yard of Tilehouse Street Meeting in Hitchin. There is a memorial stone erected in the church wall in her honor by the youths of the church a century after her death when her narrative had established her prominence in the dissenting circles. The church books of the Tilehouse Street Baptist Meeting in Hitchin also note that she contributed some £2 /15s toward the erection of their first church building in 1692. These sparse facts would suggest that she was a member of the Hitchin congregation during that period and that she had a special fondness for Mr. Wilson, its minister, as she had had for his fellow minister, John Bunyan. The stone fixed upon the wall of the meeting house reads as follows:

> Agnes Beaumont, of Edworth, Bedfordshire, (afterwards Mrs. Story) became a Member of the Church at Bedford, under the Pastoral care of the Rev. John Bunyan, October 31st, 1672. Died at Highgate, Nov. 28th, 1720, aged 68 years. And being brought to Hitchin, by her own desire, was interred in the adjoining ground. This stone was erected in 1812, in respectful remembrance of a person so justly celebrated, for her emminent piety and remarkable sufferings.

Works Cited

Armstrong, Nancy. *Desire and Domestic Fiction: A Political History of the Novel.* Oxford, 1987.

Berg, Christine and Berry, Philippa. " 'Spiritual Whoredom': An Essay on Female Prophets in the Seventeenth Century." In *1642: Literature and Power in the Seventeenth Century.* Ed. Frances Barker. Essex, 1981.

---

[12]John Beaumont Sr.'s will indicates that after settling £200 on his son William and one shilling apiece on his other surviving children, John Beaumont left Agnes "the residue" of at least £150 and possibly more.

Beaumont, Agnes. *A Narrative of My Persecution*. Ed. G.B. Harrison. Constable's Miscellany, London, 1929.

———. *Real Religion exemplified in the Singular Experience and Great Sufferings of Mrs. Agnes Beaumont of Edworth in the County of Bedford. As written by herself.* "Formerly published with several other accounts by Samuel James, A.M." Revised and published separately by Samuel Burder. London, 1801.

———. *The Singular Experiences and Great Sufferings of Mrs. Agnes Beaumont, who was born at Edworth, in the County of Bedford. As written by herself.* In *An Abstract of the Gracious Dealings of God with Several Eminent Christians, in their Sufferings.* Ed. Samuel James, M. A. Ninth edition, ed. Isaac James. Bristol and London, 1824.

Behind Mr. Bunyan. London, 1962.

Bosse, Lynda E., "The Father's House and the Daughter in It: The Structures of Western Culture's Daughter-Father Relationship." *Daughters and Fathers.* Eds. Lynda E. Bosse and Betty S. Flowers. Baltimore, 1989.

Bosse, Lynda E., and Betty S. Flowers. "Introduction," *Daughters and Fathers.* Baltimore, 1989.

Bunyan, John. "A Few Sighs From Hell." *The Entire Works of John Bunyan.* Ed. Henry Stebbing. 4 vols. London, 1862.

———. *Grace Abounding to the Chief of Sinners* and *A Relation of My Imprisonment.* Ed. Roger Sharrock. Oxford, 1962.

Chidley, Katherine. *The Justification of the Independent Churches of Christ.* London, 1641.

Damrosch, Jr., Leopold. *God's Plot and Man's Stories.* Chicago, 1985.

Demos, John Putnam. *Entertaining Satan: Witchcraft and the Culture of Early New England.* Oxford, 1982.

Ezell, Margaret. *The Patriarch's Wife: Literary Evidence and the History of the Family.* Chapel Hill, 1987.

Findley, Sandra and Hobby, Elaine. "Seventeenth Century Women's Autobiography." In *1642: Literature and Power in the Seventeenth Century:* Ed. Frances Barker. Essex, 1981.

Flandrin, Jean-Louis. *Families in Former Times: Kinship, Household and Sexuality.* Trans. Richard Southern. Cambridge, 1979.

Foucault, Michel. *The History of Sexuality: Volume 1.* Trans. Robert Hurley. New York, 1978.

Fraser, Antonia. *The Weaker Vessel.* New York, 1985.

Furlong, Monica. ed. *The Trial of John Bunyan and the Persecution of the Puritans: Selections from the Writings of John Bunyan and Agnes Beaumont.* London, 1978.

31

George, Margaret. "From Goodwife to Mistress: The Transformation of the Female in Bourgeois Culture." *Science and Society* 37 (Summer 1973).

Greaves, Richard L. *John Bunyan.* Grand Rapids, Michigan, 1989.

Heilbrun, Carolyn G. "Women's Autobiographical Writings: New Forms." *Prose Studies* 8 (1985).

Hill, Christopher. *The World Turned Upside Down.* New York, 1972.

_____. *The Experience of Defeat: Milton and Some Contemporaries.* New York, 1984.

Hinton, R. W. K. "Husbands, Fathers, Conquerors." *Political Studies* 23:3 (1967): 291–300.

Hobby, Elaine. *Virtue of Necessity: English Women's Writing 1649–88.* London, 1988.

Hopkins, James K. *A Woman to Deliver Her People: Joanna Southcott and English Millenarianism in an Era of Revolution.* Austin, 1982.

Karlsen, Carol F. *The Devil in the Shape of a Woman: Witchcraft in Colonial New England.* New York, 1987.

Keeble, N. H. "'Here is her Glory, even to be under Him': the Feminine in the Thought and Work of John Bunyan." *John Bunyan and His England 1628–88.* Eds. Anne Laurence, W. R. Owens and Stuart Sim. London, 1990.

Kolodny, Annette. "Captives in Paradise: Women in the Early Frontier." *Women's Personal Narratives: Essays in Criticism and Pedogogy.* Ed. Leonore Hoffman and Margo Cudy. New York, 1985.

Morgan, Edmund. *The Puritan Family: Religious and Domestic Relations in Seventeenth-Century New England.* Westport, 1966.

Nadelhaft, Jerome. "The Englishwoman's Sexual Civil War: Feminist Attitudes Toward Men, Women, and Marriage 1650–1740." *Journal of the History of Ideas* 43 (1982): 555–579.

Nussbaum, Felicity A. *The Autobiographical Subject: Gender and Ideology in Eighteenth-Century England.* Baltimore, 1989.

Myers, William. Ed. *Restoration and Revolution.* Dover, New Hampshire, 1986.

Owens, W. R. "Introduction." *Grace Abounding to the Chief of Sinners* by John Bunyan. New York, 1987.

Perry, Ruth. *The Celebrated Mary Astell: An Early English Feminist.* Chicago, 1986.

Pollock, Linda. *Forgotten Children: Parent-Child Relations from 1500–1900.* Cambridge, 1983.

Pomerleau, Cynthia S. "The Emergence of Women's Autobiography in England." *Women's Autobiography: Essays in Criticism.* Ed. Estelle C. Jelinek. Bloomington, 1980.

Quaife, G. R. *Wanton Wenches and Wayward Wives: Peasants and Illicit Sex in Early Seventeenth-Century England.* New Brunswick, 1979.

Rowlandson, Mary White. *The Sovereignty and Goodness of God, together with the Faithfulness of His Promises Displayed; Being a Narrative of the Captivity and restoration of Mrs. Mary Rowlandson, Commended by her to all that Desire to Know the Lord's Doings to, and Dealings with Her, Especially to her Dear Children and Relations.* Cambridge: Samuel Green, 1682; rpt. in *So Dreadfull a Judgment: Puritan Responses to King Philip's War, 1676-77.* Ed. Richard Slotkin and James K. Folsom. Middleton, Conn., 1978.

Schucking, Levin L. *The Puritan Family: A Social Study from Literary Sources.* New York, 1970.

Shammus, Carole, "The Domestic Environment in Early Modern England and America." *Journal of Social History* 19 (1980-1981): 3-24.

Sharpe, J. A. "Domestic Homicide in Early Modern England" *The Historical Journal* 24: 1 (1981): 29-48.

Spenser, Jane. *The Rise of the Woman Novelist: From Aphra Behn to Jane Austen.* London, 1986.

Spufford, Margaret. *Contrasting Communities: English Villagers in the 16th and 17th Centuries.* Cambridge, 1974.

Stone, Lawrence. *The Family, Sex and Marriage in England 1500-1800.* New York, 1977.

Thomas, Keith. "Women and the Civil War Sects." *Crisis in Europe 1560-1660.* Ed. Trevor Aston. New York, 1965.

———. *Religion and the Decline of Magic.* London, 1971.

Thompson, Roger. *Women in Stuart England and America: A Comparative Study.* London, 1974.

Tibbutt, H. G. *The Minutes of the First Independent Church (now Bunyan Meeting) at Bedford 1656-1766.* The Publications of the Bedfordshire Historical Record Society, vol. 55 (1976).

Todd, Janet. "Marketing the Self: Mary Carleton, Miss F. and Susan Gunning." *Studies on Voltaire and the Eighteenth Century* 217 (1983): 95-106.

Walzer, Michael. *The Revolution of the Saints.* Cambridge, Mass., 1982.

Whiting, C. E. *Studies in English Puritanism from the Restoration to the Revolution, 1660-1688.* New York, 1931.

The Wonderfull Dealings of God with
Mrs. Agnes Beamount, written by her self.

THE NARRATIVE OF THE
PERSECUTIONS OF AGNES BEAUMONT

The following note is prefaced to the original manuscript:

Written by one Agnes (Beaumont) of Edworth, Beds. intimately acquainted with John Bunyan, and to whose meetings she went contrary to her father's wishes, he objecting to his daughter attending such. She mentions his name in several parts of the MS.

THE LORD hath been pleased, since I was awakened,[1] to exercise me with many and great trials; but, blessed be his gracious name, he hath caused all to work together for good to my poor soul, and hath often given me cause to say it was good for me that I have been afflicted.[2] And oh, how great hath the kindness of God been to me in afflicting dispensations! In trials and temptations he never left me without his teaching and comforting presence, and I have often observed that, the more trouble and sorrow I have had either from within or without, the more of God's presence I have had; when I have been helped to keep close to him by prayer and supplication. And oh, how sweet is his presence when a poor soul is surrounded on every side with trouble! And for my part I have found trouble and sorrow; as David saith, none knoweth but God the sore trials and temptations that I have warded[3] through in my day, some outward, but more inward. O the fiery darts from hell with which my soul hath been battered! But, on the other hand, none knows but God the sweet communion and consolation that it hath pleased a gracious God to give me in many of these hours of trouble. Oh, the great consolations and enlargements of heart, with fervent desires after Jesus Christ and his grace, which hath often made me thank God for trouble when I have found it drive me nearer to himself and to the throne of his grace. The Lord hath made troublesome times to me; praying times,

---

[1]*awakened*—spiritual awakening to the grace of Christ. On the theology of rebirth see Greaves, 49–68.
[2]"It is good . . . afflicted" Ps. 119:71; "all things . . . love the Lord" Rom. 8:28.
[3]*warded*—waded.

humbling, and mourning, and heart-searching times. But one thing I have great cause to admire God's great goodness to me in, that before a trial hath come upon me I have had great consolations from God; insomuch that I have expected something to come upon me, and that [when] I had some trouble to meet with which hath often fallen out according to my thoughts, sometimes one scripture after another would run in my mind several days together.[4] That would signify something I had to meet with, and that I must prepare for a trial, which would drive me into corners, to cry to the Lord to be with me. And oh, how hath the Lord as it were taken me up into the mount, that my soul hath been so raised and comforted as if it had been out of the body for a time.[5] Many times in a day would the Lord lead me into his banqueting house, and his banner over me was love.[6] Now when I found these things in a more than ordinary manner, then I did begin to think I had something to meet with; but so long as I was kept awake in my soul and in a humble, empty praying frame, he never sent me away from the throne of grace without his presence, which hath been so sweet to me that, when I have gone away from the throne of grace, I have thought long to be there again. Oh, it cannot be expressed with a tongue what sweetness there is in one promise of God when he is pleased to apply it to the soul by his spirit. It turns sorrow into joy, fears into faith; it turns weeping and mourning into rejoicing, which, blessed be God, I have experienced these things and many more in that great fiery

---

[4]Cf. *Grace Abounding*, paras. 95, 145.
[5]Cf. *Grace Abounding*, para. 174.
[6]"Banqueting table . . . banner" Canticles 2:4.

trial concerning my father's death which now I am about to tell you of.

About a quarter of a year before God was pleased to take away my father, I had great and frequent enjoyments of God; and he was pleased to pour out a spirit of grace and supplication upon me in a wonderful manner, day and night, I may say. And, the Lord knoweth it, there was scarce a corner in the house, or barns, or cowhouse, or stable, or closes,[7] under the hedges, or in the wood, but I was made to pour out my soul to God. And sometimes before I have risen from my knees, I have been as if I had been in heaven, and as if my very heart would have brake in pieces with joy and consolation, which hath caused floods of tears to fall from my eyes with admiration of the love of Christ to such a great sinner as I was.

I have wept and cried as if I should have brake my heart-strings in sunder, only with consolation. And when some have seen me weep, they thought sorrow had filled my heart. Indeed, oftentimes I have been sinking in a sea of sorrow; but not in that quarter of the year before my father died. But some would say to me, "Agnes, why do you grieve and go crying about thus? Are you minded to kill yourself with sorrow?" when indeed my tears have been for joy and not for grief; they was sweetened with the love of Christ.

And before God brought that trial upon me, I had many scriptures that would run in my mind to signify I had something to meet with, and then it may be my heart would begin to sink; but presently I should have one promise to bear me up. I did think I had some hard thing

---

[7]*closes*—an enclosure beside a building; cf. *Grace Abounding*, Preface.

to meet with, because that scripture would often dart into my mind, "Call upon me in a time of trouble and I will deliver thee, and thou shalt glorify me."[8] Wherever I was this would run in my mind, "Call upon me in the time of trouble." Thought I this must point at something to come for now I have more comfort than trouble. And that other scripture would run in my mind, "When thou goest through the fire I will be with thee, and through the waters, they shall not overflow thee."[9] And many such scriptures that I see had bitter and sweet in them. And I often said to Sister Prudon, "I have some heavy thing coming upon me, but I know not what it will be."

And the many dreams that I had, which I believe some of them was of God. I should often dream I was like to lose my life, and could hardly escape with it. Sometimes I have thought that men have run after me to take it away; and sometimes that I was tried for my life before a judge and jury, and me thought I did escape with it, and that was all.

One dream I told Sister Prudon, which she told me of after my father was dead.[10] Me thoughts in my father's yard grew an old apple tree, and it was full of fruit. And one night, about the middle of the night, there came a very sudden storm of wind, and blew this tree up by the roots, and I was sorely troubled to see this tree so suddenly blew down.

I run to it, as it lay upon the ground, to lift it up, to have it grow in its place again. I thought I see it turned up

---

[8]"Call upon me . . . glorify me" Ps. 50:15.
[9]"When thou goest . . . " Isa. 43:2.
[10]Agnes Beaumont seems to mean that Sister Prudon reminded her of this dream after her father's death.

by its roots, and my thoughts stood lifting at it as long as I had any strength, as it lay upon the ground, first at one arm, then at another, but could not stir it out of its place to have it grow in its place again; at last left it, and run to my brother's to call help to set this tree in its place again. And I thought when my brother and his men did come, they could not make this tree grow in its place again; and, oh, how troubled was I for this tree, and so grieved that the wind should blow that tree down and let others stand. And many such things that I see afterwards did signify something.

And a while after there was to be a church meeting at Gamlinghay.[11] And about a week before, I was very much in prayer with God for two things, for which I set many hours apart day and night.

And one was that God would please to make way for my going, and make my father willing, who would sometimes be against my going. And in those days it was like death to me to be kept from such a meeting. And I found at last by experience that the only way to prevail with my father to let me go to a meeting was to pray hard to God beforehand to make him willing. And before that I had often found success according as my cries had been to God in that matter; when I have prayed hard I have found my father willing, when I have feared otherwise; and when I have not, I have found it more difficult.

And the other thing that I was begging of the Lord for was that he would please to give me his presence there at his table, which many times before had been a sweet sealing ordinance to my soul; and that I might have such a

---

[11]"Gamgey" in original ms.

sight of my dying, bleeding Saviour that might melt my heart, and enlarge it with love to him.

In those days I was always laying up many a prayer in heaven against [when] I came to the Lord's table, where I often found a very plentiful return. I could say a great deal more what I have met with, and how I have been in that ordinance, but I shall forbear.[12]

Well, it did please the Lord to grant me those two things; one in a large manner indeed when I came to the Lord's table. And the day before the meeting I asked my father to let me go to it, and he seemed as if he was not very willing; but pleading with him, I told him I would do what I had to do in the morning before I went, and come home again at night. At last he was willing. So on Friday morning, which was the day the meeting was to be, I made me ready to go. My father asked me who carried me. I said I thought Mr. Wilson,[13] who was to call at my brother's that morning as he went, and I would pray him to carry me; for my brother spoke with him the Tuesday before, who told him he had thought to call at his house on Friday morn to go with him to Gamlinghay. So my father said nothing to these things.

So when I was ready, I went to my brother's, expecting to meet with Mr. Wilson to ride behind him. And there I waited some time; and nobody came. At last my heart began to ache, and I fell a crying for fear I should not go, for my brother told me he could not let me have a horse to go for they was all at work, and he was to carry my sister

---

[12]Cf. Ebner, 60.

[13]Mr. John Wilson in 1677 became the first pastor of the Baptist church in Hitchin where Agnes is buried; like Bunyan he was imprisoned as a dissenter for preaching.

behind him to the meeting, so that he could in no ways help me thither. And it was the deep of winter, I could not go on foot.

Now I was afraid all my prayers would be lost upon that account. Thought I, "I prayed to God to make my father willing to let me go, and that I might have the presence of God in that meeting, but now my way is hedged up with thorns." And there I waited, and looked, many a long look, with a broken heart.

Said my brother to me, "Mr. Wilson said he would come this way and carry you." But he did not come. "Oh," thought I, "that God would please to put it into the heart of somebody to come this way and carry me, and make some way or other for my going." Well, still I waited, with my heart full of fears least I should not go.

At last unexpected came Mr. Bunyan, and called at my brother's as he went to the meeting; but the sight of him caused sorrow, and joy, in me; I was glad to see him but I was afraid he would not carry me to the meeting behind him; and how to ask him I did not know, for fear he should deny me. So I got my brother to ask him.

So my brother said to him, "I must desire you to carry my sister today behind you."

And he answered my brother very roughly, and said, "No, not I, I will not carry her." These was cutting words to me indeed, which made me weep bitterly.

My brother said to him again, "If you do not carry her, you will break her heart."

And he replied with the same words again, that he would not carry me, that he would not carry me. And he said to me, "If I should carry you, your father would be grievous angry with me."

Said I, "If you please to carry me, I will venture that." So with a great many entreaties, at last my brother did prevail with him, and I did get up behind him. But oh, how glad was I that I was going.

But I had been just on horseback, as I heard afterwards, but my father came to my brother's, to some of the men that was at work, and asked them who his daughter rode behind. They answered such an one, with that my father fell into a passion, and ran down to the close end, thinking to have met me in the fields, where he intended to have pulled me off of the horse's back, he was so angry, because some had incensed him against Mr. Bunyan[14]; but we was gone by first.

But to speak the truth I had not gone far behind him, but my heart was puffed up with pride, and I began to have high thoughts of myself, and proud to think I should ride behind such a man as he was; and I was pleased that anybody did look after me as I rode along. And sometimes he would be speaking to me about the things of God as we went along. And indeed I thought myself a happy body that day; first that it did please God to make way for my going to the meeting; and then that I should have the honor to ride behind him. But, as you will understand, my pride had a fall.[15]

So coming to the town's end, there met with us a priest one Mr. Lane[16] who, as I remember, lived then at Bedford,

---

[14]At this time Bunyan was a figure of some controversy; see *Grace Abounding*, paras. 306–317. On the custom of riding double see the Introduction to this edition.

[15]"Pride before . . . fall" Proverbs 16:18.

[16]As a Church of England priest, Mr. Lane would be hostile to the dissenting Bunyan.

but was used to preach at Edworth; and he knew us both, and spoke to us, and looked of us, as we rode along the way as if he would have stared his eyes out; and afterwards did scandalize us after a base manner, and did raise a very wicked report of us, which was altogether false, blessed be God.[17]

So we came to Gamlinghay; and after awhile the meeting began, and God made it a blessed meeting to my soul indeed. Oh, it was a feast of fat things to me! My soul was filled with consolation, and I sat under his shadow, with great delight, and his fruit was pleasant to my taste when I was at the Lord's table. I found such a return of prayer that I was scarce able to bear up under it. Oh, I had such a sight of Jesus Christ that brake my heart to pieces. Oh, how I longed that day to be with Jesus Christ; how fain[18] would I have died in the place, that I might have gone the next way to him, my blessed Saviour. A sense of my sins, and of his dying love, made me love him, and long to be with him; and truly it was infinite condescension in him, and I have often thought of his grace and goodness to me, that Jesus Christ should so graciously visit my poor soul that day. He knew what trials and temptations I had to meet with that night, and in a few days. Oh, I have seen what bowels of pity and compassion he had towards me, that he should give me such new manifestations of his love that very day.

Well, when the meeting was done, I began to think how I should get home, for Mr. Bunyan was not to go by Edworth though he came that way. And it was almost

---

[17]See *Church Book*, 76.
[18]*fain*: gladly, willingly.

45

night and very dirty, and I had promised my father to come home at night. And my thoughts began to work, and my heart to be full of fears lest I should not get home that night. As I was troubled to get thither, so I was to get home, but in the time of the meeting, blessed be God, it was kept out. So I went first to one, and then to another, to ask who went that way that could carry me some part of the way home; but there was nobody could supply my wants, but a maid that lived at Hincksworth, half a mile off my father's, and, the ways being so dirty and deep, I was afraid to venture behind her. But I did, and she set me down at Sister Prudon's gate.

So I came home ploshing through the dirt over shoes, having no pattings[19] on. I made what haste I could, hoping I should be at home before my father was abed; but when I came near the house, I saw no light in it. So I went to the door, and found it locked with the key in it. Then my heart began to ache with fear; for if I have not been at home, if my father had happened to go to bed before I came home, he would carry the key to bed with him, and give me it out at window. But now I perceived what I was like to trust to; but however, I went to his chamber window, and called to him.

He asked who was there. "It is I, father," said I, "pray will you let me in; I am come home wet and dirty."

Said he, "Where you have been all day, go at night"; and many such like things, for he was very angry with me for riding behind Mr. Bunyan, and said I should never come within his doors again, except I would promise him

---

[19]*patting*: a kind of overshoe worn to raise ordinary shoes out of snow or mud.

to leave going after that man; for some enemies in the town had set my father against him with telling him of some false reports that was raised of him; and they affirmed them to my father for truth, and, poor man, he believed them because such persons affirmed it. So then I stood at his chamber window pleading and entreating of him to let me in, begging and crying. But all in vain; instead of letting me in, he bade me begone from the window, or else he would rise and set me out of the yard. So then I stood awhile at the window silent, and that consideration came into my mind, "How if I should come at last when the door is shut and Jesus Christ should say to me, 'Depart from me I know you not.' "[20] And it was secretly put into my mind to spend the night in prayer, seeing my father would not let me come in. "Oh," thought I, "so I will, I will go into the barn and spend this night in prayer to God, that Jesus Christ will not shut me out at last." But these thoughts presently darted in upon my mind "No, go to your brother's; there you may have a good supper, and a warm bed, and the night is long and cold." "No," said I, "I will go, and cry to heaven for mercy for my soul, and for some new discoveries of the love of Christ." But these and many frightful thoughts came into my mind, as this, how did I know but I might be knocked on the head in the barn before morning; or if not so, I might catch my death by the cold.

At last my mind began to comply with these fears. Thought I, "It may be so indeed, it being a lone house, and none near it; and it is a very cold night, I shall never be able to abide in the barn till morning." But at last one

---

[20]"Depart from me . . ." Matt. 25:41.

scripture after another came into my mind to encourage me in that work, as that word, "Pray to thy father that seeth in secret, and thy father that seeth thee in secret shall reward thee openly";[21] and that scripture, "Call upon me, and I will answer thee, and show thee great and mighty things, and thou knowest not";[22] and many a good word beside that I have forgot. I thought I had need go pray to my heavenly father indeed.

So into the barn I went, and it was a very dark night; and when I came into the barn, I found I was again assaulted by Satan, but having received some strength from God and his word, as I remember I spoke out with these and such like words; "Satan, my father hath thee in a chain; thou canst not hurt me." So I went to the throne of grace, to spread my complaints before the Lord. And indeed it was a blessed night to me; a night to be remembered to my life's end; and I hope I shall remember it with comfort to eternity. It was surely a night of prayer, and a night of praise, and thanksgiving. The Lord was pleased to keep scares out of my heart all the night after. Oh, the spirit of faith and prayer that God gave me that night. Surely the Lord was with me after a wonderful manner. Oh, the heart-ravishing visits that he gave me. It froze vehemently that night, but I felt no cold; the dirt was frozen upon my shoes in the morning. My heart was wonderfully drawn out in prayer, and, as I was in prayer, that scripture came with mighty power upon my heart, "Beloved, think it not strange concerning the fiery trials

---

[21]"Pray to thy father . . . secret" Matt. 6:4.
[22]"Call upon me . . . answer thee" Ps.50:15.

that are to try you."²³ Oh, this word "Beloved" made such melody in my heart, that I cannot tell you; and yet the other part of the words had dread in it — "Think it not strange, concerning the fiery trials that are to try you." I see that was a great trial, my father's shutting me out of doors. I thought what could be worse to me than that, and still when I was in prayer, the same scripture would run through and through my heart; but that first word "Beloved" I thought sounded louder in my heart than all the rest.²⁴ It run very much in my mind all night; I see it had bitter and sweet in it; but to be the beloved of God, I thought that was my mercy, whatever I had to meet with. I did then direct my cries to God to stand by me and strengthen me, whatever I had to meet with. And many a blessed promise I had before the morning light. One time in the night I was a little cast down, and grief began to seize upon me. Notwithstanding God had been so good to me, I was grieved to think I should lose my father's love, for going to seek after Jesus Christ. So I went to the throne of grace again to show unto him my trouble, and I was bewailing the loss of my father's love, and saying, "Lord, what will become of me if I should fail of thy love too?" that good word darted upon my mind, "The father himself loveth you."²⁵ "Oh, blessed be God," said I, "then that is enough; do with me what seems good in thy sight."²⁶

So the morning came on, and when it was light, I peeked through the cracks of the barn door to see when my father opened the door. So at last I see him unlock the

---

²³"Think it not strange . . . trials" 1 Peter 4:12.
²⁴see *Grace Abounding*, para. 95.
²⁵"The father . . . loveth you" John 16:27.
²⁶"Do what seemeth good . . . sight" 1 Sam.3:18; 1 Chron. 19:13.

door, and when he came out into the yard, he locked the door after him, and put the key in his pocket. Thought I, this looks very bad upon me, for I knew by that he was still resolved I should not go in, though he did not know I was so near as I was. But that good word, "Beloved, think it not strange concerning the fiery trials that are to try you" still sounded in my heart.

So my father came with his fork in his hand to serve the cows into the barn where I was. And when he opened the door, he was at a stand to see me there with my riding clothes on, as I came home. I suppose he thought I had been gone to my brother's.

So said I to him, "Good morrow, father. I have had a cold night's lodging here; but God hath been good to me, else I should have had a worse." He said it was no matter. So I prayed him to let me go in; "I hope father," said I, "you are not angry with me still." So I followed him about the yard as he went to serve the cows; but he would not hear me. The more I entreated him, the more angry he was with me, and said I should never come within his doors again, unless I would promise him never to go to a meeting again as long as he lived.

"Father," said I, "my soul is of more worth than so, and if you could stand in my stead before God to give an account for me at the great day, then I would obey you in this as well as other things." But all that I could say to him prevailed nothing with him.

At last some of my brother's men came into the yard for something their master sent them for, and they went home, and told their master that their [old] master had shut me out of doors; "For she," said they, "had her riding clothes on still."

My brother hearing that was troubled, and came in haste to my father's, and he did what he could to persuade him to be reconciled with me, and to let me in; but he was more passionate with my brother than with me, and would not hear him. So my brother came to me and said, "Come child, go home with me; thou wilt catch thy death with the cold." So I bid him go home, for I see that my father was more provoked with what he said than he was with me, though my brother spoke very mildly to him; and I had a mind to stay a little longer, to see what I could do with my father.

So I followed him about the yard still, and sometimes got hold of his arms and cried, and hung about him, saying, "Pray, father, let me go in"; which I afterward wondered how I durst, he being a hasty man, that many times when he had been angry I have been glad to get me out of his presence, though when his anger was over he was as good a natured man as lived.

So I see I could not prevail with him to be reconciled with me; I went and set me down at the door; and he walked about the yard, and would not come near the house so long as I was there; and he had the key in his pocket, for there I sat at the door some time. At last I began to be faint with cold, for it was a very sharp morning, and it grieved me to be the occasion of my father's staying in the cold so long, for I saw he would not go in so long as I was there.

So I went to my brother's and they gave me something to refresh me. So when I was warm and had refreshed myself, I did desire to be retired and to be alone. So I went up into one of my sister's chambers to pour out my soul to God; for the more I met with, the more I cried to the Lord.

51

The Lord was still pleased to pour out a spirit of grace and supplication upon me, and did not leave me nor forsake me.[27]

So about the middle of the day, which was Saturday, I said to my sister, "Will you go with me to my father's, to see what he will say to me now"; and she said yes, she would go with me. So we went, and when we came to the door, we found the door locked, and my father in the house; for he would not go out, but he would lock the door, and put the key in his pocket. Neither would he go into the house but he would lock the door after him.

So we went to the window, and my sister said, "Father, where are you?" And he came to the window, and spake to us. Said my sister, "Father, I hope now your anger is over, and that you will let my sister come in." So I prayed him to be reconciled to me, and fell a crying very much, for indeed at the time my heart was full of grief and sorrow to see my father so angry with me still, and to hear what he said, which now I shall not mention; only this one thing he said, he would never give me a penny as long as he lived; nor when he died, but he would give it to them he never saw before.

Now to tell you the truth, these was very hard sayings to me, and at the hearing of it my heart began to sink. Thought I to myself, "What will become of me? To go to service and work for my living is a new thing to me; and so young as I am too. What shall I do?" thought I. And these thoughts came suddenly into my mind, "Well, I have a good God to go to still"; and that word did comfort me "When my father and mother forsook me, then the Lord

---

[27]"Did not leave me nor forsake me" Heb. 13:5.

took me up";[28] but my heart sank quickly. So my sister stood pleading with him, but all in vain. Then I prayed my father, if he did not please to let me come in, that he would give me my Bible and my pattings. But he would not, and said again he was resolved I should never have one penny, nor penny-worth, as long as he lived; nor when he died.

As I said, I was very much cast down at this. Now did my thoughts begin to work. Thought I, "What shall I do? I am now in a miserable case," for I went home with my sister again crying bitterly, for indeed unbelief and carnal reasoning was got in at a great rate, notwithstanding God had been so wonderful good to me but the last night in the barn.

So away I went upstairs to cry to the Lord that afternoon, who gave me hopes of an eternal inheritance; and I was let to see I had a better portion than silver or gold. Oh, then I was willing to go to service or be stripped of all for Christ. Now I was unconcerned again at what my father had said. I was made to believe I should never want.

So at night I had a mind to go again to my father's; "But," thought I, "I will go alone"; for I saw he was more angry with my brother that morning and with my sister at noon than he was with me. "And," thought I, "now he hath been alone one night, and hath nobody to do anything for him, it may be he will let me come in."

And so I considered which way to go. Thought I, "I will go such a byway that he shall not see me till I come to the door; and if I find it open, I will go in. He will think I will come no more tonight, and so it may be the door may be

---

[28]"When my father and mother forsake me . . . me up" Ps. 27:10.

opened. And if it is," thought I, "I will go in, let my father do with me what he pleases when I am in. If he does throw me out, he does; I will venture."

So in the evening I went; and when I came at the door, it stood ajar, with the key on the outside, and my father in the house. So I shoved it softly and was going in. But my father was coming through the entry to come out, who saw me coming in; so he came hastily to the door and clapped it to; and if I had not been very quick, one of my legs had been between the door and the threshold. So he clapped the door to with the key on the outside, for he had not time to take the key out, and then pinned the door within side, for he could not lock it, the key being on the outside of the door. So I would not be so uncivil to lock my father in the house; but I took the key out of the door and put it in my pocket, and I thought to myself, "It may be my father will come out presently to serve the cows"; for I saw they were not served up for all night. And thought I, "When he is gone up in the yard, I will go in." And thought I, "I will go stand behind the house, and when I hear him come out, I will go in; and when I am in, I will lie at his mercy."

So there I stood listening, and after awhile I heard him come out. But before he would go up in the yard to serve the cows, he comes and looks behind the house, and there he sees me stand. Now behind the house was a pond, only a narrow path between the house and the pond, and there I stood close up to the wall. So my father comes to me, and takes hold of my arm. "Hussy," said he "give me the key quickly, or I will throw you in the pond."

So I very speedily pulled the key out of my pocket and gave it to him, and was very sad and silent; for I see it to be in vain to say anything to him. So I went my way down into one of my father's closes to a woodside, sighing and groaning to God as I went along. And as I was a going with my heart full of sorrow, that scripture came in upon my mind, "Call upon me and I will answer thee, and show thee great and mighty things that thou knowest not."[29] So away I went to the woodside (and it was very dark night), where I poured out my soul with plenty of tears to the Lord; and still this scripture would often dart in upon my mind, "Call upon me and I will answer thee, and show thee great and mighty things that thou knowest not." And sometimes I should be ready to say in my heart, "Lord what mighty things wilt thou show me?" So there I remained some time, crying to the Lord very bitterly.

As any rational body must needs think, these was hard things for me to meet with. But that was a blessed word to me, "The eyes of the Lord are over the righteous, and his ears are open to their cries."[30] Oh, I did believe, his ears were open in heaven to hear the cries of a poor desolate afflicted creature, and that his heart did yearn towards me. That was a wonderful word to me, "In all their afflictions he was afflicted."[31] So staying so long, my brother and sister was much concerned for me, and sent some of their men to my father's on some errand, on purpose to see whether my father had let me come in. But they returned to their master that answer that their old master was alone; I was not there.

So my brother and some of his family went about seek-

---

[29]"Call upon me . . . marvelous things" Jer. 33:3.
[30]"The eyes of the Lord . . . their cries" Ps.34:15.
[31]"In all their afflictions . . . " Isa. 63:9.

ing for me but found me not. At last I came to my brother's, when I had spread my complaints before the Lord. And now I began to resolve in my mind what to do, for this was the case — that if I would promise my father never to go to a meeting again, he would let me come in. So, thought I to myself, that I would never do, if I beg my bread from door to door. And I thought I was so strongly fixed in this resolution that nothing could move me; whatever I met with from my father, I should never yield upon that account. But poor weak creature that I was, I was Peter[32] like, as you will hear afterwards.

Well, this was Saturday night. So when Sabbath day morning came, I said to my brother, "Let us go to my father's as we go to the meeting." But he said no, "It will but provoke him." So we did not. And as my brother and I went to the meeting, he was talking to me as we went.

"Sister," said he, "you are now brought upon the stage to act for Christ and his ways." Said he, "I would not have you consent to my father upon his terms." "No, brother," said I, "if I beg my bread from door to door." Thought I, "I do not want any of your cautions, upon that account." So we went to the meeting; but as I sat in the meeting my mind was very much hurried and afflicted, as no wonder considering my circumstances. So when it was night, I said to my brother as we went from the meeting, "Let us go to my father's." So he consented to it.

And we went and found him in the yard serving the cows, but before we came into the yard, my brother warned me again that I did not consent to promise my father to forsake the ways of God; but I thought I had no

---

[32] *Peter like*: like St. Peter, see Matt, 26:69.

56

need of his counsel upon that account. So my brother talked with him very mildly, and pleaded with him to be reconciled to me. But he was so angry with him that he would not hear him. So I whispered to my brother, and bid him go hence. "No," said he, "I will not go without you." Said I, "Go, I will come presently." But as he afterwards said, he was afraid to leave me for fear I should yield. But I thought I could as soon part from my life.

So my brother and sister went on their way home. So there I remained in the yard, talking to my father who then had the key in his pocket. And I was pleading with him to let me go in; "Father," said I, "I will serve you in anything that lies in me to do for you as long as you live and I live; and Father," said I, "I desire time to go nowhere but to hear God's word, if you will but let me go a Sabbath days to the meeting; and I desire no more. Father," said I, "you can't answer for my sins, nor stand in my stead before God; I must look to the salvation of my soul, or I am undone forever."

So he told me if I would promise him never to go to a meeting as long as he lived, I should go in, and he would do for me as for his other children; but if not I should never have a farthing.

"Father," said I, "my soul is of more worth than so; I dare not make such a promise"; and my poor brother's heart ached that he did not see me follow him. So my father began to be very angry and bid me begone, and not trouble him, for he was resolved what to do; "And therefore tell me; if you will promise me never to go to a meeting again, I will give you the key and you shall go in."

So many times together [he] held the key out to me, to

see if I would promise him; and I as often refused to yield to him.

So at last he began to be impatient; "Hussy," said he, "what do you say? If you will promise me never to go to a meeting again as long as I live, here is the key; take it, and go in"; and held the key out to me. Said he, "I will never offer it to you more, and I am resolved you shall never come within my door again while I live." And I stood crying by him in the yard. So he spoke hastily to me, "What do you say, hussy," said he, "will you promise me or no?"

"Well Father," said I, "I will promise you that I will never go to a meeting again, as long as you live, without your consent"; not thinking what dolor and misery I brought upon myself in so doing. So when he heard me say so he gave me the key to go in. So I unlocked the door and went in; and so soon as I got within the door, that dreadful scripture came upon my mind, "They that deny me before men, them will I deny before my father and the angels that are in heaven";[33] and that word, "He that forsaketh not father and mother and all that he hath, is not worthy of me."[34] "Oh," thought I, "what will become of me now? What have I done this night?" So I was a going to run out of the house again; but, thought I, that won't help what I have done if I do. Oh, now all my comforts and enjoyments was gone! In the room of which I had nothing but terror and guilt and rendings of conscience. Now I see what all my resolutions was come to. This was Sabbath day night, a black night.

---

[33]"Him that denies me . . . " Matt. 10:33.
[34]"He that forsaketh not father . . . " Matt. 10:37, Luke 14:26.

So my poor father came in and was very loving to me, and bid me get him some supper; which I did. And when I had done so, he bade me come and eat some. But oh, bitter supper to me! So my poor brother was mightily troubled that I did not come to his house. He wondered that I stayed so long. He did fear and think what I had done; but to be satisfied he sent one of his men on some errand to see if I was in the house with my father. And he returned his master that answer, that I was in the house with their old master, and he was very cheerful with me; which, when my brother heard, was much troubled, for he knew that I had yielded, else my father would not have let me go in. But no tongue can express what a doleful condition I was in, neither durst I hardly look up to God for mercy. Oh, now I must hear God's word no more. Thought I, "Oh, what a wretch am I, that I should deny Christ and his ways; he that had so often visited my soul, and had been so gracious to me in all my troubles. But now I have turned my back upon him. Oh, black night! Oh, dismal night!" thought I, "in which I have denied my dear Saviour." So I went to bed, when I had my father to bed; but it was a sad night to me.

So on the next morn, which was Monday morning, came my brother; and the first salutation that he gave me, "Oh, sister," said he, "what have you done? What do you say to that scripture, 'He that denies me before men, him will I deny before my father and the angels that are in heaven?' " "Oh," thought I, "it is this that cuts my heart"; but I said little to him only wept bitterly.

So my father coming in, he said no more, only said, "Good morrow, Father"; and went away. But I cannot express with words the dolor I was in; I filled every corner of the house and yard that day with bitter sighs and groans and tears. I went crying about as if my very heart would have burst asunder with grief and horror. But now and then one blessed promise or other would drop upon my mind; but I could take little comfort in them; as that word, "Simon, Satan hath desired to have thee that he may sift thee as wheat, but I have prayed for thee."[35] But oh, this lay uppermost, I must hear God's word no more. "Now," thought I, "if my father could give me thousands of gold what good would it do me?"

Thus I went groaning about till I was almost spent; and when my father was but gone out of the house, I made the house ring with dismal cries, but told not my grief to my brother, for I thought he would not pity me. Neither did I ever tell him what I went through upon that account. And when my father came into the house, then I would go out into the barns or outhouses to vent my sorrowful groans and tears to the Lord.

So before night, as I stood sighing and crying like a poor distracted body, leaning my head against something in the house, saying, "Lord, what shall I do? What shall I do?" Those words dropped upon my mind, "There shall be a way made for you to escape, that you may be able to bear it."[36] "Lord," said I, "what way shall be made? Wilt thou make my father willing to let me go to thine ordinances?" But if it should be so, thought I, yet what a wretch was I to deny Christ. Oh, now hopes of the pardon of my sins was worth a world; for the forgiveness of my sins was that I

---

[35]"Simon, Simon, Satan hath desired . . . " Luke 22:31,32.
[36]"There shall be a way . . . escape" 1 Cor. 10:13.

cried much for, saying, "Lord, pity and pardon, pity and pardon."

So at night as my father and I sat by the fire, he asked me what was the matter with me; for he took notice of me in what a sorrowful condition I was in all day. So I burst out crying, "Oh, father," said I, "I am so afflicted to think that I should promise you never to go to a meeting again without your consent; and the fears that I have lest you should not be willing to let me go"; and I told him what trouble I was in.

And he wept like a child.

"Well, don't let that trouble you," said he, "we shall not disagree."

At this I was a little comforted. Said I, "Pray, father, forgive me wherein I have been undutiful to you, or disobedient in anything." So he sat weeping, and told me how troubled he was for me that night he shut me out, and could not sleep. But he thought I had been gone to my brother's. But it was my riding behind John Bunyan, he said, that vexed him; for that enemy in the town had often been incensing of him against Mr. Bunyan, though sometime before my father had heard him preach God's word, and heard him with a broken heart as he had done several others. For when I was first awakened, he was mightily concerned, seeing me in such distress about my soul, and would say to some neighbors that came sometimes to the house; said he, "I think my daughter will be distracted, she scarce eats, drinks, or sleeps; and I have lived these three score years and scarce ever thought of my soul." And afterwards would cry to the Lord in secret, as well as I, and would go to meetings for a great while together, and had heard God's word with many tears. But that evil-minded man in the town would set him against the meetings. I have stood and heard him say to my father, "Have you lived to these years to be led away with them? These be they that lead silly women captive into houses, and for a pretense make long prayers";[37] and so never leave till he had set him against me and the meetings; and would I suppose counsel him not to let me go. And lately I met with a great deal from him upon that account.

Well, this was Monday night; but notwithstanding what my father had said to me, I was full of sorrow, and guilt of conscience; and my work was still to cry to the Lord for pardon of sin and to humble myself before him for what I had done. And much time I spent that night in crying to the Lord for mercy; now was I made to cry for pardon of sin, and that God would keep me by his grace for time to come, as if I never prayed before; and that he would keep me from denying of him and his ways. I see now what all my strong resolutions came to, and that I was but a poor weak creature if God did not keep me by his grace.

And the next day came, which was Tuesday, in which I still remained in a sorrowful frame, weeping and crying bitterly. But, as I remember, God brought me up out of this horrible pit before night, and set my feet upon a rock, and I was helped to believe the forgiveness of my sins; and many a good word I had come in upon my heart, which I have forgot.

But now I began to look back with comfort upon Friday night in the barn, and to think of that blessed word "Beloved," and I did believe that Jesus Christ was the same

---

[37]"These be they . . . silly women captive" 2 Timothy 3:6.

yesterday, and today, and forever.[38] But all day I spend in praying and crying to God in corners, unless it was to do my work about the house, and get my father his dinner. And he did eat as good a dinner as ever I saw him eat. Well, night came on, which indeed was a very dismal night to me, and had not the Lord stood by me, and strengthened me, I had certainly sank down under God's hand that night. But he was faithful, who did not suffer me to be tempted and afflicted above what I was able. Towards night that scripture would often run in my mind, "In six troubles I will be with thee, and in seven I will not leave thee."[39] And that was a mighty word to me, "The eternal God is thy refuge, and underneath are the Everlasting Arms."[40]

So in the evening, my father said, "It is a very cold night; we will not sit up too long tonight." He, when the nights were long, would sit up with me a candle's burning, as I have sat at spinning or at other work. But then he said he would have his supper and go to bed because it was so cold.

So after supper, as he sat by the fire, he took a pipe of tobacco. And when he had done, he bade me take up the coals and warm his bed; which I did. And as I was covering of him, them words run through my mind, "The end is come, the end is come, the time draweth near."[41] I could not tell what to make of these words, for they was very dark to me. So when I had done, I went out of the chamber into the kitchen.

---

[38]"Jesus Christ, the same today . . . " Heb. 13:8.
[39]"In six troubles . . . " Job 5:19.
[40]"The eternal God is thy refuge" Deut. 33:27.
[41]"The end is come . . . the set time is come" Amos 8:2.

Now the chamber where my father and I lay had two beds, and it was a lower room, so that I could hear my father when he was asleep as I sat by the fire in the next room; for when he was asleep, he used to snore so in his sleep that one might hear him all over the house. Now when I have heard him do so, I often took liberty to sit up the longer, where God gave me a heart to improve my time. And that night he slept very soundly as he used to do. And although he bade me make haste to bed, yet I did not, but went to the throne of grace, where I found my heart wonderfully drawn out in prayer for several things for which I had not found it in such a violent manner for some time before. And one thing that I was so importunate with God for was that he would show mercy to my dear father, and save his soul. This I could not tell when to have done pleading with God for. And that word still ran through my mind, "The end is come, the end is come, the time draweth near"; and the word, "The set time is come." But not one thought I had that it had respect to my father's death. And another thing,[42] I was crying to the Lord for was that he would please to stand by me, and be with me, in whatsoever I had to meet with in this world; not thinking what I had to meet with that night and week. But I was so helped to direct my cries to the Lord as if I had known what had been a coming upon me, which I did not. And it was a very sweet season to my poor soul.

So after a great while I went to bed, and when I came into the chamber, my father was still asleep, which I was glad of; which I often used to be, when I had sat up a great

---

[42]*another thing*: ms. reads "Anothing."

64

while, for if he happened to hear me come to bed, he would often chide me for sitting up so late.

So I went to bed, I hope with a thankful heart to God for what he had given me that night. And after I had been abed a while, fell asleep; but I suppose had not been asleep long but heard a very doleful noise. I thought it to be in the yard, not being quite awake. At last it awakened me more and more, and I perceived it was my father. So hearing him make such a doleful noise I started up in my bed.

"Father," said I, "are you not well?" And he said, "No." Said I, "How long have you not been well, pray?" Said he, "I was struck with a pain at my heart in my sleep; I shall die presently."

So I start out of my bed and slipped on my petticoats and shoes, and ran and light a candle, and came to his bedside. And he sat upright in his bed, crying out to the Lord for mercy. "Lord," said he, "have mercy on me. I am a poor miserable sinner; Lord Jesus, wash me in thy precious blood."

So I stood by him trembling to hear him in such distress of soul for Christ, and to see him look so pale in the face. So I knelt down by his bedside and spent a little time in prayer by him, so well as God helped me; and he seemed to join with me so earnestly. So when I had done, which was more than ever I did with him before, "Father," said I, "I must go call somebody, for I dare not stay with you alone"; for I had nobody with me, nor no house very near.

Said he, "You shall not go out at this time of the night; don't be afraid of me." And he still made the house ring with cries for mercy. So he said he would rise, and he put on his clothes himself. And I ran and made a good fire against [when] he came out; and he all the while cried and prayed for mercy; and cried out of a pain at his heart. Thought I, maybe it is cold that is settled about his heart, for want of taking of hot things when he would not let me come in, and had nobody to do anything for him. So I run and made him something hot, hoping he might be better. "Oh, I want mercy for my soul," said he, "Oh, Lord show mercy to me; I am a great sinner. Oh, Lord Jesus, if thou dost not show mercy to me now, I am undone forever."

"Father," said I, "there is mercy in Jesus Christ for sinners; Lord help you to lay hold of it."

"Oh," said he, "I have been against you for seeking after Jesus Christ; the Lord forgive me, and lay not that sin to my charge."

So, when I had made him something hot, I prayed him to drink some of it; and he drank a little of it, and strained to vomit, but did not. So I run to him to hold his head, as he sat by the fire; and he changed black in the face, as if he was a dying. And as I stood by him to hold his head, he leaned against me with all his weight. Oh, this was a very frightful thing to me indeed! Thought I, "If I leave him, he will drop in fire; and if I stand by him, he will die in my arms, and nobody near me. Oh," I cried out, "Lord help me, what shall I do?" Those words darted in upon my mind, "Fear not, I am with thee; be not dismayed, I am thy God, I will help thee, I will uphold thee."[43]

So after a little it pleased God my father revived again, and came to himself; and cried out again for mercy, "Lord, have mercy upon me, I am a sinful man; Lord spare me

---

[43]"Fear not . . . thee" Isa. 41:10.

one week more, one day more." Oh, these was piercing
words to me! So sitting awhile by the fire after he came to
himself, for I think he did swoon away for a time, he said,
"Give me a candle to go in to the chamber, for I shall have
a stool."

So he took the candle and went into the chamber; and I
see him stagger as he went over the threshold. So I made a
better fire against [when] he came out, and when I had
done I went into the chamber to him presently, and when I
came within the door, I see him lie upon the ground. And
I run to him, screaming and crying, "Father, Father,"; and
I put my hands under his arms, and lift at him to lift him
up, and stood lifting at him, and crying till my strength
was gone, first at one arm, then at another. As some afterwards said, my dreaming of the apple tree did signify
something of this. There I stood, lifting, and crying, till I
was almost spent and could perceive no life in him. Oh,
now I was in a strait indeed. So I see I could not lift him
up, I left him and run through the house, crying like a
poor afflicted creature that I was, and unlocked the door
to go call my brother.

Now it was the dead time of the night and no house
near. And as I ran to the door, these thoughts met me at
the door, that there stood rogues ready at the door to
knock me on the head, at which I was sadly frighted; but
thinking that my poor father lay dead in the house, I saw I
was now surrounded with trouble. So I opened the door,
and rushed out much affrighted. And it had snowed
abundance that night; it lay very deep, and I had no
stockings on so that the snow got into my shoes that I
could not run apace, and going to the stile, that was in my
father's yard, I stood crying and calling to my brother. At

last God helped me to consider that it was impossible to make them hear so far off. Then I gat over the stile, and the snow water caused my shoes that they would not stay on my feet for want of stockings; but I ran as fast as I could. And about the middle of the close, as I was running to my brother's, I was suddenly surprised with these thoughts, that there were rogues behind me, that would kill me. With that I hastily looked behind me, and those words dropped upon my mind, "The angels of the Lord encampeth round about them that fear him."[44]

So coming to my brother's, I stood crying out in a doleful manner, under his chamber window, to the sad surprising and frightening of the whole family, they being in their midnight sleep. My poor brother was so frightened that he did not know my voice. He start out of his bed, and put his head out at window, and said, "Who are you? What is the matter?" "Oh, brother," said I, "my father is dead; come away quickly." "Oh, wife," said he, "this is my poor sister. My father is dead."

So he called up his servants, but they were so frightened that they could scarce put on their clothes. And when they came down out of doors, they did not know me at first. So my brother and two or three of his men ran, and was there before me. And when my brother came into the chamber my father was risen from the ground and laid upon the bed. So my brother spake to him, and stood crying over him, but he could speak but one word, or two, to him.

So when I came in, they would not let me go in to him, for they said he was just a departing. Oh, dismal night to

---

[44]"The angels . . . fear him" Ps. 34:7.

me! Indeed, as I said, had not the Lord been good to me, I had been frighted to death almost.

So presently one of my brother's men came to me, and told me he was departed. But in the midst of my trouble I had some hopes my father was gone to heaven notwithstanding. So I sat crying in a dismal manner, thinking what a great change death had made upon my poor father of a sudden, who went well to bed and was in eternity by midnight. I said in my heart, "Lord, give me one seal more that I shall go to heaven when death shall make this great change upon me." That scripture came suddenly upon my mind, "The ransomed of the Lord shall return, and come with singing to Zion, and everlasting joy shall be upon their heads; they shall obtain joy and gladness, and sorrow and sighing shall fly away."[45] Oh, I longed to be gone to heaven I had such a sense of the work of the saints was now about in heaven. Think I, they are singing and I am sorrowing; but I see it to be a mercy that I had any hopes through grace of going thither.

So my brother, quickly after he came, sent some of his men to call in neighbors. So among the rest came Mr. Feery and his son, who so soon as they came in house, asked if my father was departed; and somebody told him yes. And he answered it was no more than he looked for. Now nobody took notice of them words till afterwards. So some women came in, who saw me set without my stockings and scarce anything on me, bewailed my sorrowful case, and the terrifying things I had met with that night.

Now this was Tuesday night my father died, and now I remember that scripture on Friday night in the barn,

---

[45]"The ransomed of the Lord . . . " Isa. 35:10.

69

"Beloved, think it not strange concerning the fiery trials that are to try you." Thought I, "I have had fiery trials since Friday night indeed"; little thinking I had as bad, or worse, to come still, though God in his infinite goodness caused it to work for good to my soul and made me say, it was good for me that I have been afflicted.

Well, that day, which was Tuesday, there was a fair at Baldocke; and this priest, Mr. Lane, that met Mr. Bunyan and me on horseback at Gamlinghay town's end, was at Baldocke that day, and told it about the fair that he had seen me behind John Bunyan going to Gamlinghay, and at the town's end there we was naught together. And, as I heard, it ran from one end of the fair to the other presently. So on Wednesday morning, the next day after the fair, when my poor father lay by the walls, came somebody in and told me what a report there was of me at Baldocke Fair. But that scripture bore me up, "Blessed are ye when men shall revile you, and say all manner of evil of you falsely, for my name sake."[46]

So the next day my brother and we concluded for burying my father on Thursday night; and he spake for wine and all things to come in on Thursday. We also invited all our friends, and relations, and neighbors to come in on Thursday; some we invited several miles about. So when this was all done and concluded of, Mr. Feery sent for my brother to his house.

So on Wednesday night my brother went. And when he came, he had him into his parlour to speak with him. So said he to my brother, "I had a mind to speak with you. Do you think your father died a natural death?"

---

[46]"Blessed are ye when men revile . . . " Matt. 5:11.

My brother was amazed to hear him ask such a question; but he answered and said, "I know he did die a natural death."

"But," said he to my brother, "I believe he did not; and," said he, "I have had my horse twice out of the stable today, to fetch Mr. Halfehead of Potten, the doctor. But, I considered, you are an officer in the town, and so I will leave it to you. Therefore, pray see you do your office."

Said my brother, "How do you think he came by his end, if he did not die a natural death?"

Said he, "I believe your sister poisoned him."

"I hope," said my brother, "we shall satisfy you to the contrary."

So my poor brother comes home with a heavy heart, for he did not know but I might lose my life, and he was very much troubled to think what I had yet to meet with. So he calls my sister upstairs to speak with her, and told her; which caused great distress in them both. And there was a good man in the town at Sister Prudon's. So they went for him, and my brother told him of this thing. So they three went up into an upper room, and spread it before the Lord. So my brother asked this man and my sister whether he had best come to my father's that night to tell me of it; and they said, "No, let her have this night at quiet." So he did not come; but that night they spent much time in prayer.

So the next morning my brother came early, and with a very sad countenance calls me up upstairs. "Sister," said he, "I must speak with you." So I went up with him into the chamber, and when he came up, he fell a weeping.

"Oh, sister," said he, "pray God help you; you are like to meet with hard things."

"Hard things?" said I. "What, worse than I have met with?"

"Yes, worse than ever you met with yet."

So he told me my neighbor Feery accused me with my father's death, and said that I had poisoned him. At the first hearing of it, my heart sank in me, and it was a very sad and sudden surprise to me. But I quickly said to him, "Oh, brother, blessed be God for a clear conscience." But although I knew myself clear in the sight of God, yet anybody must needs think these were hard things for one so young as I to meet with.

So my brother said, "I must send to Potten for Mr. Halfehead, who is a doctor and a surgeon both." And we was also first to send to all those we had invited to my father's funeral to desire them not to come till they heard further from us. So all the town, and towns thereabouts, wondered what the matter was, knowing my father did not die in debt.

So we went for Mr. Halfehead, and told him how things was; that such a one in the town, did think that I had poisoned my father. So he examined me, how my father was before he went to bed; and what supper he ate. And I told him everything that he asked me, and he seemed to be much concerned for me. And when he had viewed the corpse, he went to Mr. Feery's to talk with him, and told him he wondered he should have such thoughts of me; there was no ground for it. But he said to Mr. Halfehead, he did believe it was so.

So Mr. Halfehead saw no arguments would convince him, he came back to my brother and me, and said we must have a coroner and a jury. So I prayed him that he

would please to open my father. "Sir," said I, "as my innocency is known to God, so I would have it known to men."
"No," said he, "there is no need to have him opened."
So we desired him to come the next day to meet the
coroner and the jury; and he said he would. So now I had a
new work lay before me, and I did betake myself to prayer,
to fly to God for help, and that he would please to appear
for me in this fiery trial. I see my life lay at stake, and the
name of God lay there too; and many prayers and tears was
poured out to God, and that sweet cordial the Lord sent
me to comfort me; oh, it was a blessed promise indeed;
and blessed be God he also made it good. "No weapon
that is formed against thee shall prosper; and every tongue
that shall rise up in judgement against thee, thou shall
condemn";[47] and that word would often come into my
mind, "As many as are incensed against thee shall be
ashamed."[48]

So the next morning, which was Friday morning, my
brother sent for the coroner and jury to come that day. So
Mr. Feery, hearing my brother had sent for them, he sent
for my brother to his house, and he went. So when he
came there, said he, "I hear you have sent for the
coroner."

"Yes," said my brother.

Said he again, "I would wish you to meet the coroner at
Bigglesworth, and agree it there, and not let him come
through; for it will be found petty treason; she must be
burned."[49]

---

[47]"No weapon shall prosper . . . " Isa. 54:17.
[48]"As many as are incensed . . . " Isa. 41:11.
[49]On the patterns of domestic crime in early modern England and the rarity
of daughters killing fathers, see J. A. Sharpe.

Said my brother, "We are not afraid to let him come through."

So my brother came and told me what he said.

"Brother," said I, "I will have him come through, if it cost me all that ever my father left me; for if we should not, then he and all the world might say I am guilty indeed." Though, as I said, I see my life lay at stake; for I did not know how far God might suffer him and the devil to go. And this also troubled me, that if I had suffered, another as innocent as I must have suffered too; for Mr. Feery said that I made a hand of my father, and John Bunyan gave me counsel to poison him when he carried me behind him to Gamlinghay; that then we did consent to do it. Nay, as I remember, it was said that Mr. Bunyan gave me stuff to do it with. But the Lord knew to the contrary, that neither he nor I were guilty of that wickedness in thought, word, nor deed. But yet notwithstanding I knew myself clear, yet I must tell you, I see myself surrounded with straits and trouble; and carnal reasoning gat in. Thought I, "Suppose God should suffer my enemies to prevail, to take away my life; how shall I endure burning?" Oh, this made my heart ache at a great rate; though, blessed be God, my heart did not accuse me, in thought, word, nor deed. But the thoughts of burning would sometimes shake me all to pieces; and sometimes I should think of that scripture that would so often run in my mind before my father died, "When thou goest through the fire, I will be with thee; and through the waters, they shall not overflow thee." And then I should think this, "Lord, thou knowest I am innocent; therefore if it shall please thee to suffer them to take away my life, yet surely thou wilt be with me. Thou hast been with me in all my straits, and I hope thou will not leave me now in the greatest of all." And arguing thus from the experience of God's goodness to me in times of trial, at last I was made to believe that, if I did burn at a stake, the Lord would give me his presence. So I was made, in a solemn manner I hope, to resign myself up to God, to be at his disposing, for life or death. But still I was greatly concerned for the name of God, that is like to suffer, let it go which way it will with me; for think I, "Though it may be some will not believe it, yet a great many will; doubtless the name of God will suffer. But," think I, "I must leave it with God, who hath the hearts of all men in his hand."

So that day the coroner was to come in the afternoon, some Gamlinghay friends came to me, and they spent several hours in prayer before the coroner came, that God would please to appear graciously for me, and for the glory of his own name. So when they had done, I got into a corner by myself; for I had a great mind, to be with God alone at the throne of grace where I usually found relief, and succor, and help. And that was very much upon my heart, to cry to the Lord to give me his presence that day; so much of it that I might not have a dejected countenance, nor be of a daunted spirit before them; for I see that to be brought before a company of men, and to come before them of being accused of murdering my one father, that, although I knew myself clear in the sight of God, yet without an abundance of his presence, I should sink before them. Thought I, if they should see me dejected and look daunted, they would think I was guilty. I begged of the Lord that he would please to carry me above the fears of men, and devils, and death itself; and that he would give me faith and courage that I might look my accuser in the face with boldness, and that I might lift up my head before him, with conviction to themselves.

And as I was earnestly crying to the Lord, with many tears, for his presence, that blessed word darted in upon my mind, "The righteous shall hold on their way, and they that have clean hands, shall grow stronger and stronger."[50] Oh, I broke out with these words, "Lord, thou knowest my hands and my heart are clean in this matter." I thought it was such a suitable word, I could scarce have had the like; and the Lord made it good ere the sun went down, every little of it. So I was helped to look my accuser in the face with boldness.

So presently word was brought that the coroner and the jury were come to my brother's, and when they had set up their horses, and came altogether, they came to view the corpse. And I, with some neighbors, was by the fire; and as they passed through the house into the chamber where my father was laid out, some of the jurymen came and took me by the hand, with tears running down their cheeks, and said to me, "Pray God be thy comfort, for thou art as innocent as I am, I believe." So another would say to me, and truly I looked upon this to be a mercy to me, to see them so convinced of my innocency.

So when the coroner had looked on my father, he comes out into the house, and stood and warms himself by the fire, and with a steadfast look, looks upon me.

Said he, "Are you the daughter of this man deceased?"

"Yes, sir," said I.

"And what are you she that was in the house alone with him when he died?"

---

[50]"The righteous shall hold . . . grow stronger" Job 17:9.

"Yes, sir, I am she."

So he shook his head, which I thought his thoughts had been evil towards me and not good.

So when the jury had viewed the corpse, they went back to my brother's. And when they had dined, they sat about the business. So my brother sent for me, and I went. And as I was going, my heart went out mightily to God to stand by me; and such words as these passed through my heart, "Thou shall not return again ashamed."[51] And before I came to my brother's, my soul was made like the chariots of Aminmadab,[52] and I was wonderfully borne up, beyond what I did ask or think.

So when I came there, my brother sent for Mr. Feery and he did not come. So my brother sent again. At last he came. So then they sat about their business.

So the coroner called for the witnesses, my brother's men, that were with my father before he departed and gave them an oath; and likewise Mr. Feery was sworn to speak the truth and nothing but the truth. So, as I remember, my brother's men was examined first. So they answered to all the coroner asked them, which was this, whether they was there before my father died. And they said yes. And how long he lived after they came, and what words they heard him speak. So he had quickly done with them. Then he called Mr. Feery.

"Come," said he, "you are the occasion of our coming together, we would know what you have to say as to this maid's murdering of her father, and what ground you have to accuse her."

---

[51]"Thou shall not return again ashamed" Ps. 74:21.

[52] *Aminnadab:* Amminadib—Canticles 6:12.

So he made such a strange preamble that nobody knew what to make of it, of the difference that was between my father and I; and of my being shut out of doors; and my father's dying two nights after I came in.

And there I stood in the parlour among them, with my heart full of comfort as ever it could hold; and I was got above the fears of men and devils.

So said the coroner, "This is nothing to the matter in hand; what have you to accuse this maid with?"

But he said but little or nothing to the purpose, so that the coroner was very angry at the contrary answers that he gave him to what he asked him; but I have forgot most of his pitiful answers. But at last the coroner was very angry, and bade him stand by, if there was all he could say.

So the coroner calls me, "Come, sweetheart," said he, "tell us where you was that night your father shut you out."

Now the man that went to Bedford for the coroner had told him how all things was as they rid along.

"Sir," said I, "I was in the barn all night."

"And wast thou there alone all night?" said he.

"Yes, sir, I had nobody with me."

So he shook his head, "And where did you go the next morning?"

"Sir," said I, "I laid in the yard with my father till about nine or ten o'clock to persuade him to let me go in; but he would not."

And the coroner seemed as if he was concerned at the hearing of these things. So he asked me where I was that day.

"Sir, I went to my brother's," said I.

"And where was you that night?"

I told him that I lay at my brother's that night as my brother's servants did witness.

So he asked me when my father let me come in.

I told him it was Sabbath day night.

And he asked me if he was well, and how long it was after I came in that he died.

"Sir," said I, "it was Sabbath day night that I went in, and he died the next Tuesday night."

"Was he well that day?" said he.

"Yes, sir, as well as ever I saw him in my life, and ate as good a dinner as ever I see him eat."

So he asked me what he ate at supper.

So I told him.

He asked me after what manner he was taken, and what time.

"Sir," said I, "the manner of his being taken was in his sleep, with a pain at his heart, he said; and as to the time, it was a little before midnight. I, being in the same room, heard him groan; so I made haste to rise, and light a candle, and went to him; and he sat upright in his bed, crying out of a pain at his heart, and that he should die presently; and I was sadly frightened, so that I could scarce get any clothes on me. So he said he would rise; and I made a fire, and he sat by it, and I ran and got him something hot, and he drank a little of it, and strained to vomit and I run to him to hold his head; and he swooned away, and I could not leave him to call in anybody; for if I had he would have dropped into the fire for he leaned against me, with all his weight.

"Was there nobody in the house with you?" said he.

"No sir," said I, "nobody with me but God."

So he shook his head.

"So when my father came to himself, he said he should have a stool; and he went into the chamber, and quickly after I followed him, and he lay all along upon the ground. So I ran screaming to him, and lift at him; but could not lift him up, so left him, and ran in a very frightful condition to my brother's.

But the man that went for the coroner had told him how I frightened the family. So he said to me, "Sweetheart, I have no more to say to thee."

So next he spake to the jury, and when they had given up their verdict, and all was done, he turns himself to Mr. Feery. Said the coroner, "You that have defamed this maid after this manner, you had needs make it your business now to repair her reputation again. You have taken away her good name from her, and you would have taken away her life from her if you could. She met with enough I think," said he, "in being in the house alone that night he died. You need not have added this to her affliction and sorrow. If you should have given her five hundred pounds, it would not make her amends."

So the coroner comes to me, and takes me by the hand, "Come, sweetheart," said he, "do not be daunted, God will take care of thy preferment, and provide thee a husband, notwithstanding the malice of this man; and bless God for this deliverance, and never fear but God will take care of thee. But I confess these are hard things for one so young as thou art to meet with."

So I had a mind to speak to the coroner and jury before they departed; "Sir," said I, "if you are not all satisfied, I am freely willing that my father should be opened. As my innocency is known to God, so I would have it known to you, for I am not afraid of my life."

"No," said he, "we are all well satisfied of thy innocency; there is no need to have him opened. But," said he, "bless God that the malice of this man broke out before thy father was buried."

So the room, where we was, was very full of people, and it seems great observation was made of my countenance, as I heard afterwards. Some gentlemen that were upon the jury said, they should never forget me, to see with what a cheerful countenance I stood before them all. They said I did not look like one that was guilty. I know not how I looked, but I know my heart was full of peace and comfort. All the jury was much concerned for me, though carnal men, and it was observed they sat with wet eyes many of them while the coroner was examining of me. And indeed I had cause to thank God, that he did convince them of my innocency. And I heard that a twelvemonth after they would speak of me with tears.

So then we sent to invite all our friends to come to my father's funeral on Saturday night. So now I thought surely my troubles and trials upon that account was at an end. I thought Mr. Feery had vented all his malice now; but he had not, he was resolved to have another pull with me. Seeing he was prevented of my life, he did attempt to take away what my father left me; for he sent for my brother-in-law, that had married my own sister, from my father's grave, and told him how things was left as to my father's will, and that my father had given her but a shilling to cut her off. And he told him he could set him in a way to come in for a part, which my brother was glad to hear of.

Now my father's will was made three years before he died, and Mr. Feery made it. And then he put my father on to give me more than my sister because of some design

81

that he had then, but afterwards when I came to go to meetings he was turned against me. And I did not know but that will that was made then had been altered; but it was not. So the next thing I was to meet with I must speedily resign up a part of what my father had left me to my brother-in-law, or else he would sue me. So this was a new trouble to me; I was threatened at a great rate. Mr. Feery said, "Hang her, don't let her go away with so much more than your wife." So to law they would have gone with me presently but I agreed to give my brother threescore pounds for peace and quietness.

Well, one great mercy the Lord was pleased to add to all the rest; he was pleased to keep prejudice out of my heart to this man. And the Lord did help me to cry to him in secret, with many tears, for mercy for his poor soul; and I longed after the salvation of it, and I begged forgiveness of and for him for what he had done against me.

Well, about a month after my father was buried, another report was raised of me. It was hotly reported at Bigglesworth that now I had confessed that I had poisoned my father, and that I was quite distracted. And there the people would get together to tell one another this news.

"But is it true?" said some. "Yes, it is true enough," said others.

So I heard of it. "Well," thought I, "if it please God to spare me, I will go the next market day to let them see." I was not distracted, I was troubled that the name of God did suffer. So when Wednesday morning came, I made me ready to go to Bigglesworth, and it was very sharp and cold; it was frost and snow, but I could not be contented without going. The Lord was wonderful good to my soul, that morning; that scripture ran mightily through my mind as I was going to the market, "Blessed are ye, when men shall revile you, and say all manner of evil of you falsely for my name sake; rejoice and be exceeding glad, for great is your reward in heaven"; and that word, "As many as are incensed against thee shall be ashamed." I was very comfortable in my soul, as I was going, and when I came there.

So I went to my sister Everads to rest me; and when it was full market, I went to show myself among them. And when I came into the market, the poor people could not follow their business that they were about, but I think I may say almost all the eyes of the market were fixed upon me. Here I could see half a dozen stand together, whispering and pointing at me; and there I should see another company stand talking together. So I walked through and through the market. Thought I, "If there were a thousand more of you, I could lift up my head before you all." I was very cheerful, for I was very well in my soul that day.

So a great many came to me and said, "We see you are not distracted." And I saw some cry, and some laugh. "Oh," thought I, "mock on; there is a day a coming will clear all." That was a wonderful scripture to me, "He will bring forth thy righteousness as the light, and thy brightness shall be as the noonday."[53] Thus I have told you of the good and evil things that I met with in that dispensation. I wish I was as well in my soul as I was then.

***

---

[53]"He will bring forth thy righteousness" Ps. 37:6.

The following notes are added to the original manuscript: —

her name Agnes.

Edworth where Agnes lived 3 miles from Biggleswade.

Rev. John Bunyan, named by the writer as the minister she heard, was born at Elstow near Bedford 1628; had been a soldier in the parliamentary army; 1655 he was admitted a member of the Baptist meeting at Bedford and was soon after chosen their pastor and for preaching the gospel was sent to Bedford jail where he was kept 12 1/2 years; he died in London 1688 age 60.

N.B. —In the jail he wrote his Pilgrim's Progress.

In the other manuscript (Egerton 2128) these concluding paragraphs are added:

After this report there was another, raised in another place in the county, and that was, *Mr. Bunyan was a widower, and he gave me counsel to poison my father so that he might have me to be his wife, and this we agreed upon as we rode along to Gamlinghay.* And truly this did sometime make me merry, as other things did make me sad, and not long after it was said, *we were married,* but they were mistaken for he had a good wife before.

I could not but tell this news to several myself, and it did serve to divert me sometimes.

Now I thought surely *Mr. Feery* had done, but the next summer after my father died, there happened to be a fire in the town, and nobody could tell how this fire came. But *Mr. Feery* did secretly affirm it, that I did set the house on fire. But the Lord knows I knew nothing of it till I heard the doleful cry of fire in the town.